V. 25

KU-477-304

A World to

Leslie Lyall

J B Buell

*Singapore became a Republic in
1965*

OMF BOOKS
237 West School House Lane
Philadelphia Pa. 19144

Inter-Varsity Press
and
Overseas Missionary Fellowship

© Leslie T. Lyall

Inter-Varsity Press
Inter-Varsity Fellowship
39 Bedford Square
London WC1B 3EY

Overseas Missionary Fellowship
Newington Green
London N16 9QD

First edition June 1972

ISBN 0 85110 361 8

Printed in Great Britain by
C. Nicholls & Company Ltd
The Phillips Park Press, Manchester
Set in Linotype Granjon

Contents

Acknowledgments

Many people, engaged in missionary work throughout the world, and too numerous to name individually, have been involved in the preparation of this book. The author's thanks are due to those who saw the original outline of the book and made useful comments and suggestions to him. Special thanks are due to those who supplied the basic information for the 'Problems to Ponder' at the end of each chapter, and to Mr Michael Bradshaw for his help and ideas on the presentation of facts and figures, especially in the first chapter and the statistical tables at the end of the book.

Biblical quotations are from the Revised Standard Version of the Bible, copyrighted in 1946 and 1952, unless otherwise indicated.

Introduction

Two thousand years ago Jesus Christ declared liberty to the captives and commissioned His followers to claim the world for Him. 'Ask of me, and I will make the nations your heritage, and the ends of the earth your possession' (Psalm 2:8) were words quoted of the Risen Lord in Acts 13:33. By His death and resurrection He had defeated the great usurper and was soon to charge His church to possess His possessions and to enter into His heritage. 'Go therefore and make disciples of all nations' (Matthew 28:19).

In 1848 Karl Marx and Friedrich Engels drew up a manifesto in Brussels which concluded with the stirring words: 'Workers of the World, unite! You have nothing to lose but your chains. You have *a world to win*.'

Christianity and Communism thus share the vision of liberation and world conquest. But the Christian church has been desperately slow to catch fire, and in 1972 the world's population remains largely in the dark as to salvation through Christ, while the Communist movement has captured one third of the world in just half a century. The race is on. Moreover we live in a revolutionary world and time is running out. John F. Kennedy said in a TV address in 1960: 'It is time for a new generation of leadership, to cope with new problems and new opportunities. For there is *a new world to be won*.'

Christians, fired with Christ's love and compassion and empowered by His Spirit, can still more than match the zeal of the Communists for world conquest. This is the moment for the total mobilization of all Christian believers to fulfil our

Lord and Captain's last command to 'Go into all the world and preach the gospel to the whole creation' (Mark 16 : 15).

1
The world's dimensions – a call to evangelize

We live in a nightmare world and, especially for giant nations such as China and India where famines and floods are endemic and where food has always been insufficient to feed the people adequately, the prospect of a larger and larger population must be a haunting nightmare indeed. As it is, between 20,000,000 and 30,000,000 in the world die of starvation and malnutrition every year.

Professor Jacques Piccard, the marine explorer, said in October 1971 that eight million tons of oil pouring into the ocean every year and other pollutions are rapidly killing off plankton, the vegetable first stage in the chain feeding all marine life. Consequently the world's oceans may be dead by the end of the century. And scientists speaking on a BBC 'Horizon' programme in March 1971 about man's abuse of the resources of his own world, the poisoning of the rivers and oceans with insecticides, the dumping of industrial waste and the pollution of the atmosphere by the internal combustion engine, also predicted a certain ecological disaster before the end of the century unless immediate united action is taken by the nations of the world to prevent it. The hour may already be too late.

Raymond Ewell, editor of *Population Bulletin,* writes: 'If present trends continue it seems likely that famine will reach serious proportions in India, Pakistan and China in the early 1970's followed by Indonesia, Iran, Turkey, Egypt and several other countries within a few years, and then followed by most of the other countries of Asia, Africa, and Latin America by 1980. Such a famine will be of massive proportions affecting

7

hundreds of millions, possibly even billions of persons. If this happens, as appears possible, it will be the most colossal catastrophe in history.' This may be far too pessimistic a forecast, but the fact is that, despite the 'green revolution' and the development of 'miracle rice' and other high-yielding strains of cereals, world population is now out-racing food production at the rate of 2 to 1 per year. 'The stork passed the plough' in 1963, an event more ominously significant than the atomic bomb. The UN Food and Agricultural Organization is attacking this stupendous problem but, some say, forty years too late.

Thus the humanity of man and of his societies is threatened by a greater variety of destructive forces than ever. And may not the judgment of God on a world that rejects His authority work through 'natural' disasters? If all this sounds like a doom-watch prediction, is it not at least likely that the prophets will prove to be right? On the other hand, man has succeeded in the past in overcoming very great problems and if a stabilization of population can be achieved this would provide real hope for a solution of the other threats of starvation and pollution. But everything calls for a far greater sense of urgency both for the world's politicians and for the Christian church. A revolutionary young generation is challenging the very structure of the world's economy and is demanding immediate change.

Population

The fact is that in no previous century has the population of the world so much as been doubled. While in the twentieth century it promises (or threatens!) to quintuple itself and is increasing at more than 60,000,000 every year. There were 3,700,000,000 living persons in the world in early 1971 (UNESCO figures). By 1980 with 90,000,000 births in excess of deaths, there will be over 4,000,000,000. At the end of the century the population of the world, if it can survive, will at an average 2% per annum growth rate be more than 6,000,000,000 and may well be 7,500,000,000. Moreover, the fastest population growth is in the 'Third World' regions of Africa, Asia and Latin America. There the percentage annual growth is 2.3% in Asia, 2.7% in Africa and 2.9% in Latin

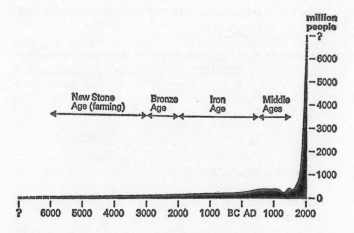

Fig. 1. The dramatic growth in world population since 1800 AD compared with the stable population of the previous 8,000 years.

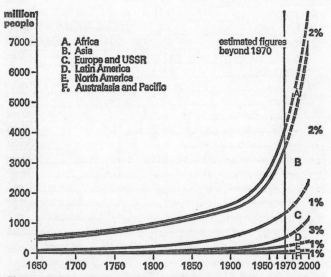

Fig. 2. World population (1968) by continents. Percentages at right-hand side are current annual rates of population increase.

9

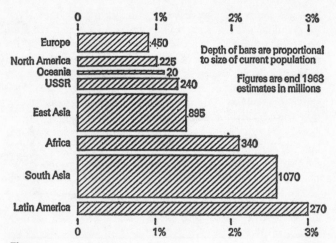

Fig. 3. Growth in world population. Percent increase calculated end 1967 – end 1968.

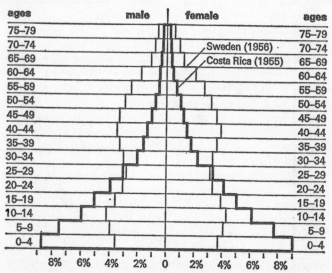

Fig. 4. Population structure. Age-sex pyramids for a typical developing country (Costa Rica) with over 50% of the population under 20, and a developed country with a population which is becoming 'top-heavy' (Sweden).

America compared with only 0.8% in Europe. By 2000 AD, of 4,000 million Asians 1,700 million will be Chinese! With the extraordinary growth of population we are confronted with the novel situation that 50% of the world's people are now under 21, and 37% are under 15 (in the 'Third World' it averages 42%). In Singapore ('instant Asia') 75% are under 21. Thus youth predominates. Youth are not the leaders of tomorrow – they are already the leaders of today. 'When Jesus saw the crowds, he had compassion on them' – physically hungry, yes, but also spiritually lost to God. There is something worse than the physical destitution which can be publicized through press photographs of emaciated children and starving old women. Unfortunately it is impossible to photograph the tragedy of spiritual destitution – men, women and children 'without God, without Christ, and without hope'. Why is it that we are more moved to shame and compassion by the physical needs of our fellowmen than by their spiritual need?

The Good News

These millions are all 'God's offspring' – His children by creation, the objects of His love. For them He has provided a way of access to Himself, a sacrifice for sin and a free forgiveness in Jesus Christ, whose death and resurrection were events in time more astounding than any other event before or since. President Nixon was wide of the mark when he declared the first landing on the moon to be the most epoch-making event in history. That claim is for ever reserved for the crucifixion and resurrection of the Son of God. Nothing will ever surpass those stupendous events in significance.

Salvation through the Lord Jesus Christ is the Good News which He Himself commanded the church to publish to all mankind. God 'desires all men to be saved and to come to the knowledge of the truth' (1 Timothy 2:4). But this task can never be completed once for all; it must be undertaken afresh in every generation. Moreover the task becomes more formidable in every generation as the number of people increases. And so God is for ever urging His church out into all the world to make disciples of all nations. There is nothing parochial or sectional or racial about the gospel; it alone meets the deepest need of all men of whatever race or culture. The gospel is vital and essential to all, whether rich or poor, educated or illiterate, Brahmins or outcasts, Spanish conquerors or Inca Indians, the religious or the irreligious, humanists or Communists. Man was made by God having a soul that needs God and makes him capable of knowing God. Without a living faith in God life in the present becomes meaningless, a fact which men and women of every culture are today discovering through bitter experience. And without faith in Christ men also face a future judgment beyond death.

Everyone must cling to the hope that by the end of the century a solution will have been found for the international disputes that cause wars, that the problems of hunger and starvation will have been overcome, that a cure will have been found for killer diseases like cancer and coronaries, that environmental pollution will have been ended and that international relations will have been stabilized. But, for Christians, the most pressing question of all is, 'Will all the people of the world have been reached with the saving message of the gospel by 2000 AD?' This goal should be at the heart of all that the church is planning in the decades immediately ahead.

The church's task

In the first century the task of evangelizing the world with its then estimated 250,000,000 inhabitants must have seemed a colossal if not an impossible one. Yet our Lord initially committed it to a small handful of simple men who daringly stepped out in obedience, determined to fulfil it. Today, in the last third of the twentieth century, the task is infinitely more formidable.

On the other hand, though Christians are still a minority, the church is a living reality in virtually every land and Christian believers are numbered by the millions. What God requires of His whole church now, as of the early Christians, is total obedience to His command to evangelize the world and at any cost. We have no options. This has always been and remains the *raison d'être* of the church both in Africa and Asia, as in Britain or America. She obeys or she rebels. As Phillips Brookes once said, 'The Church must evangelise or fossilise!'

Motive :!! obedience & need

and that applies to the church in Asia, Africa, Latin America as well as elsewhere. The prime motive for evangelism, therefore, is obedience; the crying need of the world constitutes the call of God only in a secondary sense. But what kind of a world do we live in? How great is its need?

Urbanization

Crowding more and more human beings into our planet creates new and insoluble problems, as well as exacerbating the terrifying problems we already face. Take one current phenomenon. The world is steadily becoming one enormous township. In 1800 the population of the world was 97% rural. In the 1940s the annual urban growth rate was 3%; it rose to 4% in the '50s and in the '60s it was 6%. Today 40% of the world's people live in towns and cities.

This movement from the country to the cities is history's

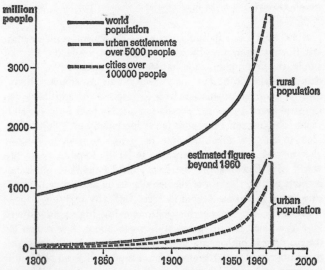

Fig. 5. Urbanization. The proportion of the world population living in urban settlements has grown from 3% in 1800 to 14% in 1900, 27% in 1950 and 40% in 1970. Those living in large cities (over 100,000 people) have risen from under 1% of the total in 1800 to 5% in 1900 and 30% in 1970.

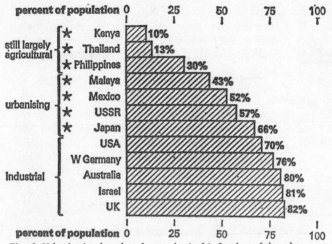

Fig. 6. Urbanization by selected countries (1960). In view of the subsequent growth in urbanization the figures for the countries marked * will have increased greatly.

greatest migration. In some countries the entire population is fast flowing away into the towns and cities. In Japan, for example, the urban population has leapt from 40% to 70% in one decade. Today in no less than seven South American nations, over 50% of the population lives in large towns and cities. In England over 80% of the population already lives in towns and cities. The State of Singapore is predominantly city. Soon after 2000 AD 90% of mankind may be living in cities or towns. Tokyo, with 11,400,000, is reputed to be the largest city in the world. But Ben Wati of the Evangelical Fellowship of India predicts that by the end of the century India alone may have 20 cities with 20,000,000 people in each. But why this migration?

Cities are the magnet for youth seeking higher education. Having gained their degrees and qualifications, few return to the rural areas but remain in the towns where alone remunerative employment and the amenities of modern life can be found. But cities as industrial complexes are the most powerful magnet for men and women looking for better wages and higher living standards. They too are swelling the urban population of the world.

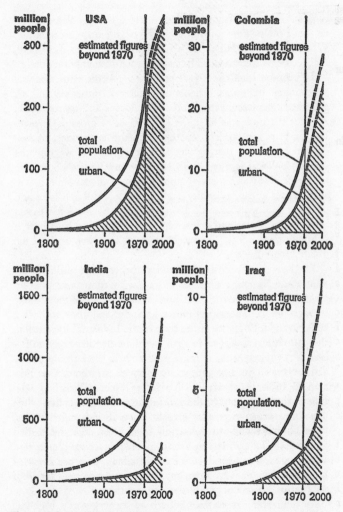

Fig. 7. Urbanization. Compare the proportions of the populations living in towns in 1900, 1970 and 2000 AD. Also compare the actual numbers of town-dwellers for each of these dates.

Twentieth-century cities follow a uniform pattern the world over. Only the colour and the features of the people thronging their streets and the languages of the exotic shop signs distinguish them one from another. Acute urban problems facing us in Britain are spreading with frightening acceleration. Whether it is Birmingham or Bangkok, Lima or Liverpool, Nairobi or Nottingham, all follow a similar contemporary design – the familiar high-rise offices and flats, and the same essential government buildings, schools and colleges, museums and art galleries, cinemas, theatres and opera houses and sports stadia. All face the problems of traffic congestion, of gross overcrowding, of grinding poverty and terrible slum conditions, of syndicated crime and blatant vice. In the cities, too, we find the greatest political ferment, with Marxists and Radicals operating most effectively. This social upheaval on a global scale inevitably causes great inner-city turbulence, painful tensions and growing insecurity. People living in huge concrete blocks experience loneliness and a loss of identity which in turn have a dehumanizing effect. The world is facing an urban crisis of the greatest magnitude.

Yet it is in the cities that today the teeming millions for whom the Saviour's heart is moved with compassion are increasingly to be found. If our Lord were to describe them today it might be as builders without a foreman, or typists without a supervisor. In England, at the time of the Industrial Revolution, the church largely failed to read the signs and neglected to follow the people into the cities. The church in these revolutionary times cannot afford to repeat the mistake anywhere. One mission in India is reported to have 'lost' 10,000 Christians who moved from rural churches into Calcutta. The fact is that while exploding urban networks present unparalleled opportunities, most churches and missions find themselves, like the baffled government authorities, in a trap, unable to move, ill-prepared to deploy men and funds into new situations. They are stranded high and dry, miles from the masses of the people and far from the centres of influence in the emerging nations.

 In Singapore, in a new suburb of twenty-storey high-rise buildings containing over 36,000 housing units or 200,000 people, a plot of land for a church building would be quite

16

prohibitive in price for a small Christian group. But one Chinese Christian leader has the vision of a number of house-churches in every block of flats on the estates; these would provide Sunday schools as well as social and community services for all. Already one such church centre exists in one block of flats. And this may be a pattern for all new housing estates. 'If we lose the battle for the cities,' declares Eugene A. Nida of the American Bible Society, 'we shall never recover from the blow.' Trail-blazers through the concrete jungles of the world to reach their burgeoning millions are in short supply. There are more heathen in a single block of flats in Singapore than in the average tribe in the jungle. *(S'pore)*

Rural population

Despite the rapid process of urbanization which is changing the shape of the world, the majority of the world's population remains, for the present, predominantly rural, especially in countries like Thailand, India or Kenya. Even in 1980 more than half the world's population in each continent will still be living in rural communities of less than 20,000 people. Of India's 800,000 villages only 100,000 have resident Christians. In Thailand 90% of the population lives in small rural communities of less than 3,000 inhabitants and only one in every 1,000 of the nation's 33,000,000 is Christian. So the task of rural evangelism cannot be neglected in favour of the cities, though it will be better done by national churches rather than by foreign missionaries.

Tribal communities, mostly living under primitive conditions and many without a written language, make up less than 5% of the world's population. Government policies, generally speaking, aim at integrating these tribal groups into the national life and culture as soon as possible. But for some years to come pioneers prepared for rugged and simple living will be needed to reach the present generation of tribal folk with the Good News and to provide for them at least some portions of the Bible in their own language (*cf.* Chapter 6).

The drift of educated young people away from the rural areas to the towns is a feature which makes church-building in the former very difficult; no sooner are young potential leaders converted than they tend to move away seeking education or employment. Nevertheless, the work of rural evangelism the world over is still one of major importance. Our Lord has compassion on these multitudes too, for they are as sheep without a shepherd.

Pioneer evangelism

Modern exploration has left very few regions of the world unreached. The age of the venturesome 'pioneer missionary' has virtually come to an end. But the pioneer spirit will find new forms of pioneering just as difficult and as beset by obstacles as the old, though not of the same geographical or physical nature. Today's pioneer must penetrate – that is the operative word – unevangelized segments of society: the industrial working-class in Japan or Italy, for example, the social 'upper-crust' in Argentina or Nepal, the religiously inaccessible in Muslim or Buddhist lands. The church cannot afford to be merely on the periphery of society. Above all, the modern pioneer must at all costs reach the crucially important 20,000,000 student population of the world in a far more effective way and with a far larger effort than at present. There are 2,500,000 university students in Asia alone. Student workers in the IVF tradition are obviously one way to help meet the need. The methods of Campus Crusade (of American origin) involve a far larger international staff of evangelists and they lay less emphasis on the internal autonomy of student organizations. But the large-scale penetration of universities all over the Third World by foreign Christian students who will witness strongly within the universities as students could also prove to be a most effective method. It will need vision and courage and almost certainly financial assistance to take advantage of such opportunities.

René Padilla, Latin American student leader, has this to say: 'The failure of the church in the evangelization of the educated is apparent to the most inexperienced observer. This is certainly so, at least in the case of Latin America. Here, where the Protestant movement is said to be increasing at a rate which surpasses the rate of over-all population growth, the presence of the educated in the churches is proportionately so negligible as to be virtually non-existent.' Or Eugene A. Nida: 'The history of the modern missionary movement is marked by an almost complete neglect of students and professionals. With a few notable exceptions the large majority of missionaries have orientated their work primarily to savages in the jungles and secondarily to peasants in the rural areas and the under-privileged in the cities, to the total abandonment of a whole segment of the population – the educated.' But J. S. McCullough of the Andes Evangelical Mission (Bolivia) has said recently: 'Our accent is changing. We have always been a pioneer mission, but now we are pioneering in the cities and among the youth of Latin America.' And that goes for missions in every continent.

Travel
Year after year the travel agencies offer more and more exotic package tours to every conceivable corner of the world. The Polar route shuttles passengers from London to Tokyo overnight. Jumbo jets hustle tourists to the land of the Incas in a matter of hours. Soon the Concorde may be taking passengers across the Atlantic and back, for lunch and a shopping spree in New York. People living in the heart of Borneo who have never seen a train or a car are already quite familiar with the giant planes flying overhead as well as the tiny Cessna planes which make regular visits to the local air strip, bringing the messengers of the gospel to teach them more about God and how to be good disciples of Jesus Christ. Few areas of Asia, Africa or Latin America are any longer physically remote whether by scheduled air lines or through missionary plane services. There is now no valid excuse for failing to reach every creature with the gospel message in our own generation.

Single world culture
Universal radio communications and the growing prevalence of TV, the almost identical educational syllabus followed throughout the world and the rapidly-increasing tempo of international travel are creating a uniform world – a single world culture. Youth the world over follows the same fashions in dress, admires the same pop stars, and suffers from the same terrific

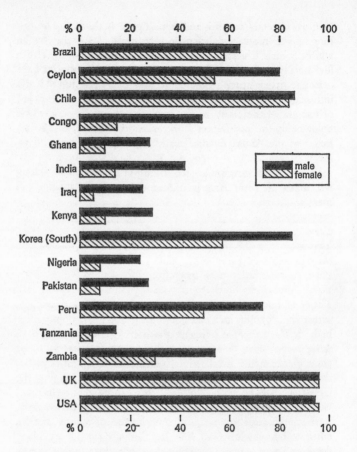

Fig. 8. Literacy (1967). Figures for selected countries, with male/female distinction. Many countries are now making intensive efforts to overcome the low literacy, particularly amongst women.

pressures of a fast-changing society. Communication satellites are already being used for mass education in under-developed countries. Literacy is on the increase, but electronics are leapfrogging the class room and illiterates are receiving their education less from books than from the transistor radio. If education is regarded as essential to all mankind, is not salvation in Jesus Christ equally essential? In Christ God met the world. In Christ men can meet each other and Jesus Christ is the point of conjunction. Tensions, violence and frustration are the *milieu* within which Christians must render clear witness to God's love and grace in Jesus Christ (*cf. World Vision*, Sept, 1968).

In the first century the Roman roads of Paul's day and the universal use of the Greek language facilitated the rapid spread of the gospel; similarly in the twentieth century modern technology makes possible not only mass education but also the early evangelization of the world — given the men and the means.

Marshall McLuhan prophesies an 'explosion of the eye' which will make the revolutions of history look tame. 'The giving to man of an eye for an ear by phonetic literacy is,' he contends, 'socially and politically, probably the most radical explosion that can occur in any social structure. Yet it is inevitable, because literate and pre-literate cultures are bound to increase their contacts with each other.'

No closed doors
The Christian world has become familiar in recent years with the dangerous talk of 'closed doors'. Such talk, however, may betray an old-fashioned 'colonial' viewpoint. Closed to whom? Presumably to the unwelcome emissaries, the 'neo-colonialists' of the West! But if 'closed doors' in Burma have shut out the Western missionary, they have also shut in the Christian church which remains as a witness to the living Christ behind those doors. Since missionaries were asked to leave by the government the number of baptisms annually has been maintained and even increased, while there are more students in the theological colleges than ever. Wonderful things have happened in the Southern Sudan since the doors closed to foreigners. One day we shall learn details of the great things God is doing in China behind doors closed only to outsiders.

Doors are never closed to the gospel if the gospel remains inside and so long as Christian radio can penetrate beyond man-made barriers or curtains. Moreover prayer, through which powerful forces are released within the church wherever she is found, knows nothing of 'closed doors'. And because the Risen Christ is the Lord of open and closed doors (*cf.* Revelation

3:7), when the doors of China and Burma were closed to foreigners, other doors, until then closed, wonderfully opened even to Westerners; to Laos, to Cambodia, to Vietnam and to Nepal. And they are still opening one by one into those few remaining strongholds which in past centuries have been closed to the gospel. Furthermore, the lure of advanced education is bringing citizens of Somalia, of Afghanistan, of Bhutan, of Tibet, of Arabia and other 'closed' lands to study in Europe and America where they are being introduced to the One who is the Way, the Truth and the Life. And we must never assume that doors which are at present closed to outsiders will not open again when God's time comes.

Meeting the need

Our Lord's story of the Good Samaritan unquestionably teaches that the need constitutes an obligation. As far as the Samaritan was concerned, the need was a call to act. And he obeyed. We feel nothing but contempt for the two pious religionists who did not see things that way and hurried by on the other side to some other less demanding religious duty. In Thailand, 999 people in every 1,000 are not Christians. In Japan there are still 99,000,000 unconverted Japanese and 110,000,000 unconverted Indonesians in Indonesia. How can we pass these multiple millions by?

But the need of the world today – material or spiritual – no longer consists merely in the multitudes who live out of reach of the gospel, very great though that need is. An appeal based on them alone does not stand up to the test of Scripture. In a secular post-Christian world the need is on every one's door step, not least here in post-Christian England or America. Then second or third generations of Christians in Korea or Kenya also need to be evangelized, because theirs is often merely a nominal profession of faith. But perhaps the greatest need lies in the growing but biblically illiterate churches in places like Indonesia, Brazil or India. Local churches, fully equipped by the Holy Spirit and not the traditional foreign missionary societies, must be seen today to be the real key to the evangelization of the world. But only thoroughly Bible-based and revived churches can carry out their mission to the unreached millions.

It follows that, as far as external assistance is concerned, it is not primarily foreign evangelists that are needed. For them the language and culture will always impose severe limitations on their effectiveness. What is urgently and primarily needed are teachers (who are also soul-winners) to teach the Bible both at every level of church life and in Bible schools or theological colleges.

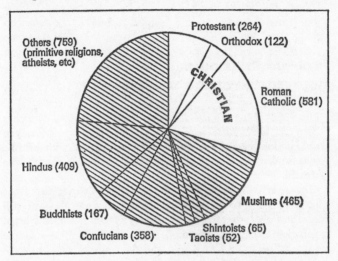

Fig. 9. World religions (1966). Figures in millions. It is emphasized that these are estimated figures and subject to variation according to source.

The optimism of the Victorian hymn-writers, or even that of the world missionary leaders of the Edinburgh Missionary Conference of 1910 who anticipated the early evangelization of the world, can no longer represent the outlook of today. World evangelization is no longer the sole prerogative of 'foreign missions' as it was once seen to be, but it is primarily the responsibility of the church within every national boundary. However, in this task the churches of the world must help one another and most national churches welcome the assistance of Christians from other lands. World mission is the mission of God through His whole church in the power of the Holy Spirit to the whole world.

BIBLIOGRAPHY

The Meaning of the City by Jacques Ellul (Eerdmans, 1970).

Evangelical Strategy in the New Towns by an Evangelical Alliance Study Group (Scripture Union, 1971).

Pollution and the Death of Man by Francis A. Schaeffer (Hodder and Stoughton, 1970).

Mission in a Dynamic Society by J. Rossel (SCM Press, 1971).

Problems to ponder
Reaching students in a Hindu university

Background situation

The Hindu university of Benares is residential with about 10,000 students, the men mostly living in hostels of 300 to 500 each.

The Arts College students are local. The Science and Engineering and Medical students are drawn from all parts of India and are better educated, speak English well, and are, superficially, secular in outlook.

Materialism has a strong grip and the students' one concern is to escape from the sea of poverty and unemployment around them. Many would like to study abroad.

Due to past strikes which have closed down the university, politics at the student level are banned.

There is little cultural life and most students, though nominally Hindus, are apathetic towards religion.

There are fifty Christians, almost all from Kerala in South India. But Christianity is regarded as Western and the fact that most of its propagators are foreigners confirms this.

One of these foreigners (Mr X) decides to become a student for the purpose of taking a two-year post-graduate course in Indian philosophy.

The objective

Not merely to distribute Christian literature, form good personal relationships, or even lead a few individuals to Christ.

The ultimate aim (and there are only two years in which to achieve it) is to establish a permanent Christian witness in this Hindu university – an ongoing, outgoing, expanding group which will make a growing impact on a wider and wider segment of the university.

How would you go about it?

Possible alternative methods

Do you begin with the many or the few?

Do you begin with your neighbours in the hostel or with those who appear most promising?

Do you begin with the students or with the lecturers?

Do you start with Bible study or by showing Christian social concern?

Do you begin by emphasizing prayer or activity?

Do you hold meetings on the campus or outside it?

(These six questions could be used in a discussion group before reading on.)

Case History

Mr X (ex-Cambridge University) takes up residence in a hostel, knowing he is there only for a short time. Previous attempts by foreigners, including a Japanese Christian, to get something started had failed. A permanent work must centre around an Indian or Indians, not the prestigious foreigner. In making contact with the Christians – a seemingly obvious beginning – Mr X finds them proud of Syrian Christianity (from Kerala in South India), whether Orthodox, Roman Catholic or Reformed, but seeing little point in Bible study.

Mr X, however, starts a Bible study and thus discovers two or three students who truly know Christ, but are afraid lest an open witness may isolate them from their 10,000 fellow students. It becomes increasingly clear that the group mentality ensures that only a Christian group will make any progress.

Mr X therefore decides to start a weekly church service outside the university to attract more Christians. But he soon discovers that this satisfies their sense of duty as Christians and thus has an adverse effect on the Bible study group, which consequently dies out. Neither the Bible class nor the service results in any headway with the Christians. The apparently strategic points and the likely growing-points fail to coincide and Mr X's problem becomes increasingly acute.

The distribution of Christian literature also misfires. There is no-one to follow up those who show an interest and there is no-one to explain the gospel to Hindu readers who merely select what appeals to them from the literature received.

At the end of two years, the Christians were still held back by their friends. Two Hindu students came to know Christ but were too individualistic to mix with other Christians. Nor did they reproduce spiritually among their own friends. Instead, both failed their exams! And so the hoped-for dynamic group failed to materialize.

Self-criticism

Mr X finds it difficult to see what could have been done differently. Ideally, he could have persuaded a young Indian believer – lecturer or student – to enter university at the same time. Two are better than one.

Mr X feels now that he should have concentrated at two points: in spending more time with the South Indian Christians and helping them to witness to their Hindu friends; this would have given them boldness and might have led to the formation of a group. Secondly, Mr X, who lived in a different hostel from the Christians, feels he should have been more open with his immediate neighbours in his own hostel and allowed his life to back up his words as evidence for his beliefs.

Conclusion

Missionaries in India are up against millennia-old strongholds. Only the use of spiritual weapons can pull down those strongholds. But how much do we know in practice about their use?

2
The church in the world –
a universal reality

Lester Pearson, Canadian Prime Minister in 1969, once said: 'We have been very slow – I hope not fatally so – to recognise the revolutionary nature of the changes that have taken place in the world in the last fifty years.' These words apply not least to the Christian.

1910 – 1970

At the historic world-wide missionary conference held in Edinburgh in 1910, in the heyday of Western colonial expansion and before the first of two tragic world wars had shattered the imperial dream, missionary statesmen looked out from their Christian citadel in the West over a pagan world, but a world which their optimism expected soon to become Christian through the influence of Christian colonization in Asia and Africa. (They ignored Latin America, which many of them regarded as already 'Christian'.)

In Europe and North America the church in the Edwardian era was at the height of its power and popularity. Elsewhere in the world it was considered scarcely to exist! The church therefore clearly saw it to be the white Christian's burden to evangelize 'the heathen' and to extend the frontiers of the Christian church world-wide. Many conceived their Christian duty to go further and to include spreading Western or Christian civilization with the gospel. But in 1910 these tasks were still, generally speaking, in their pioneer stage.

Sixty years later the picture is profoundly different. The imperial dream has been finally shattered. Imperialism and colonialism, instead of proving to be the allies of evangelism, came to be regarded after the Second World War as its enemies. The church in the Third World is today acutely embarrassed by any past association with either and is trying to live down and out-live the commonly-held view that Christianity was in some way a part of the 'imperialist plot' to dominate the world – 'the spearhead of cultural imperialism'.

A world-wide church

Nevertheless, whether with the aid of or in spite of colonial expansion, the Christian church has in these sixty years become a world-wide church. In 1971, as the last resistant strongholds have yielded to the messengers of Christ, the church is a universal reality. Bishop Stephen Neill has expressed it in these words: 'It is only rarely possible in the history of the Church or in the history of the world to speak of anything as being unmistakably new. But in the twentieth century one phenomenon has come into view which is incontestably new – for the first time there is in the world a universal religion and that the Christian religion!' This fact is the measure of the extraordinary success of Christian missions during these sixty years. True, the churches in some areas of the world are numerically small and uninfluential, but elsewhere they are large, continually growing and a powerful social and spiritual force. The churches of India, China, Indonesia and Latin America have long since developed well-qualified leadership, while African churches are following close behind.

Thus the primary goal of missions – often perhaps a more theoretical one than a real one – has been largely achieved. Urged hastily forward, it is true, by nationalistic pressures, the churches of the world have seized the autonomy they have long been promised. Under national leadership many of them have developed a mature sense of responsibility. And in some parts of the world remarkable church growth has been the result.

Church growth

Significantly it is in the continent overlooked by the Edinburgh Missionary Conference, on the ground that (in a Roman Catholic sense) it was already Christian, that the young Protestant

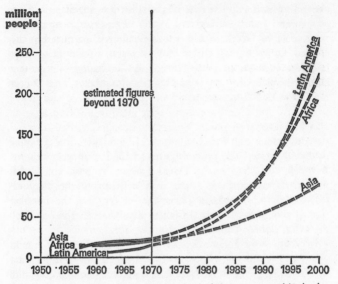

Fig. 10. Church growth. Projected growth of Christian communities in the developing continents at the following rates: Asia 5%, Africa 8%, Latin America 10%.

churches are experiencing the fastest church growth seen any-where in the world, viz. 10% per annum as compared with a normal population growth of 2.9%. Inevitably, faced as they were with bitter opposition, the Latin American churches ini-tially made slow progress. Even in 1936 there were only two and a half million Protestants in the whole continent. In 1970 this figure had increased to 15,000,000 in a total population of 300,000,000. In Brazil the Protestant community has grown from about 30,000 in 1900 to 10,000,000 or so today, nearly 4,000,000 of whom are communicants. Similar spectacular growth is taking place in Chile. In both cases Pentecostal move-ments account largely for the growth. 'This is the greatest day of harvest the church has ever had,' writes one Latin American leader. By 2000 AD there could be 50,000,000 Protestant Chris-tians in Latin America, most of them Pentecostal.

The African continent south of the Sahara is experiencing a similar phenomenon. The Christian community as a whole is expanding uniformly at twice the rate of the natural growth of population increase and in 1968 Protestants numbered 21,708,000. In Northern Nigeria alone church membership increased 117% during the civil war years – good news that failed to reach the newspaper headlines. In Central Nigeria the church is increasing by 70,000 baptisms annually. The Congo for Christ Campaigns of 1966 won 10,000 for Christ and made a powerful impact on a country only recently involved in civil war and attempted revolution. 15,000-strong Christian 'demos' parading along the main boulevards of the biggest cities dramatically illustrated the growing strength of the churches there. According to statistics by David Barrett, by 2000 AD, if the present trends continue, Africa may well become the home of 300,000,000 to 400,000,000 Christians, or 60% of the population, giving it the largest Christian population in any one continent (*cf. Church Growth Bulletin,* May 1964).

In Asia, only Indonesia can match such figures. Church growth in recent years in South-East Asia, including Indonesia, has been 25% annually. But here again economic, social and political factors as well as religious ones have led to a remarkable growth among the Indonesian churches since the end of the Second World War, and particularly in the last decade, when the Christian community has grown from about 4,000,000 to nearly 7,000,000 approximately, in a population of 120,000,000. Among the Karo Bataks of Sumatra sixty new churches came into being and 30,000 converts were baptized during 1968 and the remarkable increase has continued since then. Similar spectacular growth has taken place among the Toradjas of Central Sulawesi. These are both animistic races, but even among the Muslim Javanese there is today a church membership of about 130,000 – the largest church in the world made up of former Muslims.

Korea opened its doors to the gospel only about eighty years ago, yet today there is a Christian community of about 3,000,000, or 10% of the entire population; surely another dynamic and growing church. To quote Bishop Stephen Neill again: 'We discern the beginning of the landslide through which in many parts of the world hundreds are being turned into thousands and thousands into millions.'

One fact must not be overlooked; many of the fastest growing churches are outside the traditional denominations and have never been under the control of any missionary agency. The very 'foreignness' of Western missionary societies and the frequently dominating character of Western missionaries have driven many Africans in particular into independency, where they have been able to develop more genuinely indigenous expressions of Christianity, often, unfortunately, at the expense of truth. China was more fortunate in the indigenous churches which had their birth there and the errors and extremes of the African prophetic sects were largely avoided. Indeed, in retrospect it can be said that probably the healthiest and most spiritual churches of China, although they owed much to Missions, were entirely Chinese led and had moved quite outside the denominational and interdenominational mission orbits. The same would be true of some modern movements in India.

Growth uneven

However, church growth is by no means uniform throughout the world. In Western Europe and North America church membership is in serious decline. Europe, indeed, needs to be re-evangelized. In most Communist lands the church is just holding its own, though in China it has been forced completely underground. Where Islam prevails, except in Indonesia, churches are very small indeed and have a struggle to survive. In India, South-East Asia and Japan the churches are making only small headway against Hinduism, Buddhism, Communism and nationalistic sects. In 1900 the Christian population of the world, including all branches of the Christian church, was 38%; in 1950 it had dwindled to 30%. The figure for 1970 was 26%. If these trends continue the figure could be as low as 10% by the year 2000. With a world population growth of 62,500,000 annually, or 183,000 daily, the church must step up its present growth rate considerably if it is to keep pace with the over-all population growth.

Service

Evangelical churches are not only concerned with evangelism and church growth. They are to a varying degree interested in social service, not as a means of reforming society and changing the world, for only God can do that through the work of His Holy Spirit, but as a genuine expression of care and concern for bettering the human lot of their fellowmen. They desire peace and justice but will work for these things only in God's way – through prayer, through personal and corporate influence and through action dictated by God's Word alone. Education and medicine have always had a prominent place in the mission of the Western churches and the younger churches of the Third World have been eager to continue these ministries. African leaders in Nigeria and the Congo have shown great enthusiasm for schemes to improve agriculture as a means of helping the churches to become more financially viable. In Southern Mexico Indians have been encouraged to develop rural crafts and taught improved methods of terracing the mountainsides. The younger churches have also adopted other forms of social service and are enthusiastically involved in many branches of Christian service activity.

Church-centred thinking
The dominating theme of the Bible is the redemptive purpose of God – in the Old Testament through Israel His chosen race, and in the New Testament through His spiritual Israel, the church. The church has always been and is central in the plan and purpose of God for the world and the basic unit of the church is the congregation of believers in a particular place – the local church. When, in the seventeenth and eighteenth centuries, the churches failed in their outreach to the world, God brought into being as a result of the Evangelical Awakening the present-day missionary agencies. But should these agencies be seen as anything more than temporary phenomena? Has the time not come to restore the primary emphasis on the church as the evangelizing agency rather than the missionary society? There are those who would say No, and argue that the younger national churches are still too weak to assume full responsibility and that time has not yet come to dismantle the missionary structures.

The church, the Body of Christ

In answer to this it must be recognized that the church of Jesus Christ has always been, from apostolic times, a mixture of weakness and strength. This is still the reality today all over the world. The older churches of the West are not necessarily strong and the younger churches of the world are by no means always weak. Where once the church was strong, namely in Europe, now it is strangely weak. Indeed the centre of gravity of the Christian church numerically speaking has already shifted from Europe and North America to the Third World. But a newly-gained autonomy or independence does not in itself indicate spiritual strength, nor does a numerically large membership, as in Korea or Chile.

Fire and zeal are certainly found in Latin America and East Africa. Depth and spiritual maturity are surely characteristic of Christian literature in Great Britain. For evangelistic gift the church might look to Asia, while organizational skill and drive are the contribution *par excellence* of North America. We recognize these sources of strength where we find them, but in the very same areas equally great weaknesses are also apparent. So, in its joint mission to a godless world in every continent, the universal church needs the contribution which every continent can bring. The world-wide Body of Christ is composed of many members, each with differing functions.

While this is true on a global scale, it is equally true within any one continent or country. The apostle Paul insists that within this Body there is no distinction of nationality or race – only variety of gift. Hopefully, we in the West are beyond the stage when we think of 'aid' from the 'older' or 'stronger' churches of the West being extended to the 'younger' or 'weaker' churches elsewhere. Such aid, especially when it was material, was often irresponsible, weakening and pauperizing. It is only when we conceive of full partnership within the Body of Christ and the proper exercise of all its varying gifts that *mutual* aid becomes a reality. In rendering aid – and this is not merely, or even primarily, financial – there must be a full sense of stewardship in money, talents and time. It is not just a case of churches either giving or receiving gifts, but of all sharing God's varied gifts through His church for the promotion of the growth of the whole Body. Members of His Body wherever they are need to lose sight of the distinction between 'foreign' and 'national' and to learn respect for the contribution which all can make towards the effective functioning of the whole.

Church/mission relationships

This at once leads us to consider the greatest issue facing mission organizations at the present moment in time; namely, how in the new situation which is still developing to spell out the ideal relationship between the old missionary society and the new responsible Third World churches. The paternalistic relationship is, if it still survives (and alas it does here and there), an anachronism, and a crippling anachronism at that. But what has succeeded it? The dismantling of missionary structures (except at home) and the total integration of expatriate Christian envoys into the life of the churches, as soon as they have reached a maturity capable of sustaining it, is undoubtedly the goal at which to aim. The oldest foreign mission in Zaire, for instance, is the Regions Beyond Missionary Union, which has completely merged its identity in the 'Association of Evangelical Churches of the Lulonga'. This is one example among several in Africa and in Latin America. But they are notable exceptions. Nevertheless, all 'foreign missions' must as soon as possible come to terms with reality.

Theodore Williams, a prominent Indian leader, has written: 'If there will always be a place for the foreign missionary in any country, what is his role to be? Obviously he cannot be the representative of a foreign enterprise, whether it be a missionary society or some isolated cause of his own, however successful either may appear to be. The foreign missionary must become a member of the national church and make his contribution as a member of the national church.' Writing in *The Church of England Newspaper* on 13 November 1970, Bishop Stephen Neill had this to say of the traditional missionary 'fellowships': 'Any attempt to create another and more intimate fellowship within the Church is certain to be harmful and is certain to be bitterly resented by the Christians of the other race. . . . The loyalty of a missionary to the country and to the Church which he serves must be total and unconditional. His immediate fellowship is with the people of that country, in special intimacy, naturally, with those among them who are Christians. This is part of the price that has to be paid for missionary service; it does demand the sacrifice of much that is familiar and precious.' But this goal remains very much in the future in the case of most missions, particularly of those serving immature churches. Meanwhile full partnership in responsibility in a common task seems to be the interim pattern.

The Wheaton Congress of 1966 declared that 'the proper relationship between churches and missions can *only* be realised in a co-operative partnership. . . . The missionary society exists to evangelize, to multiply churches and to strengthen the existing churches. Therefore we recognize a continuing distinction between the church established on the field and the missionary agency.' It is doubtful if this distinction can any longer be justified in the light of Scripture and also if the national churches will continue to tolerate it indefinitely. It has been a valuable interim system, but the time has surely come to move on to face the issue of true integration. It is not possible for a foreign missionary agency to integrate with a national church. It is possible only for individual expatriate workers to integrate with local churches. And this should be the ideal. A distinction will still be necessary between the missionary agency in its country of origin, *e.g.* United Kingdom, USA, Australia, *etc.* and in its place of service. There must always be an agency or society structure in the country of origin for the purpose of disseminating information, recruiting personnel and raising funds. The missionary agency is a necessary link between the churches of different nations and it would possibly be fatal, as far as missionary zeal is concerned, to wind up mission boards in the countries of origin. But on the field of service mission structures should be giving way to church structures.

The Three-Self Formula (viz. to establish self-supporting, self-governing and self-propagating churches) had considerable value at an earlier stage of church development overseas, but today is no longer an appropriate guide to mission/church relationships. The whole idea of self-hood is foreign to the New Testament concept of the Body of Christ. In any country, or in any local church, members from the host country or guests

35

from any other country must be able to work in harmony, each exercising his particular God-given gifts for the building up of the Body and in the outreach of that Body to the community around.

The issue is no longer one of nationality. In many British churches West Indian and Asian members are taking their place as deacons and church officials. For many good reasons the top leadership will normally be exercised by nationals of the country who should take the lead at every level of decision. But expatriate workers need not be excluded from subsidiary leadership – *i.e.* in the spheres of education and medicine, when their gifts qualify them for it. (There are spheres of work in Great Britain, especially in the immigrant field, but not at all excluding the ordinary churches, where we sorely need the gifts and talents of African, Asian or Latin American Christians.) But the Afro-Asian churches are faced with a colossal unfinished task of evangelism and church planting. Congresses on evangelism in recent years held in Singapore, West Africa, India, the Philippines and in Thailand have given evidence of the willingness of Afro-Asian national Christians to assume full responsibility for evangelism in their own areas. But they would be the first to acknowledge their limited resources in personnel and money and they desperately need Christians from other lands as fellow-workers in a common task. These must be men and women who will go in the spirit of the servant, stripped of an erstwhile arrogance and sense of superiority and ready to exercise their gifts and ministry, whether as ordained or lay members of the community, in the service of the church; *i.e.* in equipping each local church for the work of the ministry of evangelization (Ephesians 4:12). The Third World churches are saying to those who might come to help them: 'Don't pressure us; don't steam-roller us; don't take us over; but do come and join us in church-based evangelism and church-orientated mission.'

It is important to note that, seen in this light, the old distinctions between the members of a missionary society and Christians in secular employment overseas, who could well be called CSOs or 'Christians in (secular) Service Overseas' (*cf.* VSOs), become blurred. Both stand on common ground in relation to the church in the country where they serve and of which all are members.

It therefore seems right for the Christian leaders in the Third World, rather than for the missionary societies, to define clearly what the needs of their own countries are as they see them, and for them to extend a welcome to all whom they would invite to join them in their task, that is the task of the whole church.

But let there be no false illusions; the relationship between a responsible national church and its expatriate members will never be an easy one. Christians from lands where the traditional concept of the church is a static one will soon discover the tension created in a situation where the Holy Spirit has imparted to the church a dynamic understanding of the church-in-mission. The ordained man may not at first see how his own ordination can find a place in the differing church structures. Is he really willing, when it comes to the crunch, to take a back seat and to allow Asian or African brethren to take the lead even when he sometimes finds himself in disagreement with some aspects of that leadership? (*Cf.* Chapter 7.)

As to church structures, there will surely need to be a continuing study of traditional patterns and the evolution of new ones in the developing situation in the world. The traditional Western structures are rightly being called in question and sometimes rejected as belonging to an alien culture. But what should take their place? At the Congress on Evangelism in Manila the Filipinos were asking themselves, What is the authentic form of Christianity for the Philippines? The Filipino church does not want to cut its links with the wider church, but the speakers showed a determination to find an authentic Filipino expression of the gospel which would not be a pale reflection of an American model. Arsenio Dominguez spoke eloquently when he said, 'I must recognize my oneness and complicity with the Church of the world. No Christian is an island. Christ's Church in the Philippines should be concerned with the mission and role of the whole Church. The problems of evangelicals anywhere should be our problems. The Church under persecution in other places is our concern. We are part and parcel of a truly ecumenical body in the different hues and colours of redeemed humanity. We have a world responsibility.

We are catholic because we recognize our universal brotherhood as God's children in Christ. But catholic or universal without ceasing to be Filipino. And proud in serving God according
to our ways and culture.'

Church unity
The maturing churches of the world are showing a growing
concern for Christian unity, both those under the influence of
the Western originated World Council of Churches and those
within the evangelical sphere. The ecumenical movement has
achieved a world-wide influence and, because of its appeal for
unity in place of the denominational diversity introduced by
foreign missionaries, seems to many nationals, including evangelicals, to make sense. The movement, therefore, is strongly
conservative, theologically speaking, in some areas, though such
areas are rare and becoming rarer. The World Council of
Churches tends to use its funds to provide advanced theological
education for national clergy as a means of strengthening support for the ecumenical movement among the national
churches. In many countries the national Christian councils, associated with the World Council, are widely accepted by national Christians. Evangelicals therefore would do well to avoid
a purely negative reaction against this massive challenge.

Christian unity is a good thing and true Christian unity
should be vigorously promoted. The Church of South India,
formed in 1947, was a pioneer experiment which has solid
achievements to its credit. It is a growing church. More recently the Church of North India has come into being. The
Evangelical Fellowship of India brings together the evangelical churches and organizations of that country and, like the
Church of North India and South India, is under Indian
leadership. Similar situations are developing in Africa and in
Latin America. Unfortunately, the polarization of the national
Christian Councils and the Evangelical Fellowships continues.
Both movements evidence a strong and universal desire for
a greater unity among Christians, but the grounds on which
such unity is possible are not agreed. There are grave
dangers that Western Christians may pass on to the national
churches their own patterns of separation, whereas, left to

38

themselves, these churches would forge a true unity in Christ.

It is true to say that the churches of the Third World now deeply resent the introduction of denominational divisions with the gospel, even though they have long since accepted the divisions and in many cases become more sectarian than their tutors. Nigerian students in a British college, however, were emphatic that it is only the missionaries who are preventing different groups of African Christians from uniting on a solid biblical basis. It is time for evangelical organizations to take a more positive lead in encouraging the greatest possible unity of fellowship and action among all evangelical Christians, churches and fellowships the world over. But John Mackay's words should also be heeded: 'An obsession with unity for its own sake instead of unity for mission is the error of ecumenicalism. There is less and less motion outwards and onwards towards the frontiers. Ecumenicalism becomes instead, increasingly, a motion towards the realization of an ordered ecclesiastical structure.' Evangelicals should most certainly unite, but theirs should be united action for the evangelization of the world.

Finally, to sum up this chapter, it cannot be stated too emphatically that the evangelistic dimensions of the Christian church are both to the ends of the earth and to the end of the age. The church must always be, wherever it is, a responsive, responsible and reproducing church involved in world mission, outward-reaching and forward-looking to the return of Christ, when at last the evangelizing task of the church will be completed – and only then.

BIBLIOGRAPHY

How Churches Grow by Donald A. McGavran (World Dominion Press, 1960).

Church Growth and Christian Mission edited by Donald A. McGavran (Harper, 1965).

Understanding Church Growth by Donald A. McGavran (Eerdmans, 1970).

The Story of the Christian Church in India and Pakistan by Stephen C. Neill (Eerdmans, 1970).

Schism and Renewal in Africa by David B. Barrett (Oxford University Press, 1968).

Church Growth Bulletin (Church Growth Institute, Fuller Theological Seminary, Pasadena, California).

Problems to ponder
Christian education as missionary work

General considerations

1. In a world where literacy used to be generally very low, Christian missions saw it to be their duty to contribute towards the education of the young generation – at least until governments of developing countries could provide their own adequate educational system for all.

2. Missions have realized that a church, to be a strong church, must be literate; in particular, the leaders must be well educated. This was a strong argument for Christian education.

3. Education has featured largely in the missionary programmes of India, China, Africa and Indonesia, a large proportion of the total budget and a considerable percentage of the missionary personnel being involved.

Has this emphasis on education proved itself to be worth while?

1. Rufus Anderson of the American Board Mission and a well-known missionary statesman in the nineteenth century decided in 1856 to close all the mission schools conducted by his mission for the past twenty years because they had not materially contributed to the building up of the churches.

2. The five Christian universities and numerous Christian high schools of China were first-class institutions from an educational point of view and so attracted the cream of China's students. But it was a policy of the Chinese government to restrict religious activities in such schools and so it was possible to pass through them without discovering what Christianity was really about or even to gain a false view of it. Thus Christian institutions featured largely in the programme of Christian missions but did not make a correspondingly large contribution to providing strong, spiritual Christian leadership in the churches. They may, indeed, have trained as many Communist leaders as Christian !

3. Many educationalists strongly believed that Christian schools should not be used to proselytize non-Christian pupils.

A missionary principal of a large boys' school in Sumatra said in 1951: 'I don't aim to make Christians out of these Muslim boys – just to make them better Muslims!'

The problem

It is still true that illiterate Christians will never build strong churches. Education for Christian children is essential. If the state fails to provide it, then the church must do so. But should Christian schools admit non-Christians? If so, are Christian schools the place in which to engage in evangelism (or proselytism) among the non-Christian students? Many Christian leaders think not. By what standards can one assess the value of education in relation to the large sums of money necessarily spent on it?

What do you think? (Discuss before reading further.)

The Indonesian case

In the era of Dutch imperialism, the East Indies were an integral part of the Dutch Empire. The Dutch Reformed Church was the national church.

Schools were therefore both government and church schools and subsidized by the government. Even now, under an independent government, little distinction is made between non-Christian and Christian schools in the matter of subsidies.

Christian schools play an important part in the educational system into which they are fully integrated and follow curricula set out by the government. They are administered and staffed entirely by Indonesian Christians and fully integrated into the national culture.

Little attempt is made by the Indonesian Government to interfere with the distinctive character of the schools; consequently teachers and pupils do not feel at any disadvantage as compared with those in non-Christian schools.

In some areas, Christian schools have higher educational standards and achieve better examination results than other schools, due to the superior dedication of Christian teachers. Consequently, non-Christian parents are often anxious to place their children in Christian schools.

In Indonesia each educational institution is required by law

to provide Religious Instruction for two hours each weeek·
Islam for the 85% of Muslim pupils and Christianity whenever
the numbers of Christian pupils justify it and where there are
teachers (often local pastors) able and willing to teach it. (Most
are diffident and reluctant.)

Objectives of Christian education in Indonesia
1. Pre-evangelism in a hostile and resistant Muslim society.
General education opens the closed minds of Muslims and dis-
poses them (unlike illiterate Muslims) to consider unfamiliar
ideas and viewpoints.
2. The impartation of secular knowledge from a Christian
point of view. Christian norms and values predispose young
people to think in a Christian manner.
3. The training of potential Christian teachers to serve the
church where ministers are often too few or inadequately educated.
4. Direct evangelism, by offering close contact with young
people and introducing them to church activities. In one area,
the percentage of non-Christians in Christian schools was as
follows: Primary 70–80%; Junior High School 50%; Senior
High School 10%.

Problems
The key to success in the Indonesian Christian education is
dedicated Christian teachers. But . . .
1. Salaries are inadequate and extra work undertaken by
many teachers to supplement their income limits their partici-
pation in extra-curricular Christian activities.
2. Many Christian teachers lack both ideas and training for
Christian service among school children.
3. Many Christian teachers are themselves only nominal
Christians.
4. There is a possibility of future pressures for the admission
of more and more non-Christians into Christian schools.
5. Many children in Christian schools are baptized (after instruction) because it is the 'done thing' and because their friends
are. Moreover, the churches are not always discriminating
about whom they baptize. So that nominalism in the church

is a danger unless RI is in the hands of well-trained and fully-committed Christians.

What results of Christian education can be shown?

An estimated 70–80% of all non-Christians turning to the Christian faith in Indonesia have been through Christian schools.

A Christian teacher training school in Solo (Java) before the last war produced scores of Christian graduates who today hold influential posts in government and education fields. Many from hostile Muslim homes were sent to this Christian college by ambitious parents.

An alternative to Christian schools

To establish hostels in educational centres, staffed by Christians, for high school and university students from rural areas, providing for them a supervised Christian home from home. One such hostel in Jogjakarta (Java) run by a Dutch engineer before the war produced many Christians who later held influential key positions in society.

Is there room for missionaries?

Education in Indonesia is a very significant field for well-qualified and experienced Christian educationists, who are more than welcome by the Indonesian churches in the field of teacher training and the organized supervision of school programmes.

Expatriate educationists have produced a syllabus and teaching manuals for RI teaching in all Indonesian primary schools and have conducted courses to train teachers in the use of these aids.

3
The world as it is –
the ugly facts

'The whole world is in the power of the evil one' was John's startling announcement to first-century Christians (1 John 5:19). In the book of Revelation the apostle elaborates this theme and sees the church in the world as violently opposed by Satan whose programme is to deceive the whole world and to destroy the church (Revelation 12). The apostle Paul earlier describes the church as engaged in a life-and-death struggle with Satanic forces on a global scale (Ephesians 6:12). And even before that our Lord had warned His followers that in a world in which Satan reigns as its prince and its god they would always be as sheep among wolves (Matthew 10:16). It is impossible to exaggerate the fiercely antagonistic nature of the human society in which the church everywhere must maintain her witness and fulfil her multiple tasks.

War
War has always been a terrible feature of our world. The manifestations of anti-war sentiment are stronger and more widespread than ever before. World wars have devastated the earth and its people, each more devastating than its predecessor. The next such major war will doubtless be a nuclear one in which the human race could destroy itself. This prospect alone is proving to be a powerful deterrent to recruiting for overseas service. A spirit of nuclear pessimism prevails among much of the youth of today and even Christian youth seems to be, perhaps unconsciously, infected by it. For if the world is soon to blow up, what is the use, they say, of considering a life of service overseas?

But civil wars, as in Nigeria or Vietnam, and small-scale international wars, as between Israel and Egypt and her Arab allies, also constitute a grave threat to international peace. The world-wide activity of the church is inevitably affected as a result – often curtailed and sometimes brought to a complete standstill. In the Congo rebellion and in the Nigerian civil war the churches suffered sadly as property was destroyed and Christians were killed or driven into the forest. In Vietnam more than twenty years of warfare have imposed tremendous strains on the people and severely limited the activities of the local Christian congregations, which, with their leaders, live in constant danger and fear of death or capture.

But even the tragedy of war has under the divine sovereignty its positive benefits; the failure of false religions to provide security or comfort in time of upheaval and danger often leads to a greater awareness of need and an increased openness to the gospel. This has been markedly so in Vietnam, where many have been dislodged from their ancestral shrines and spirit houses to become more responsive to the Good News. In Tibet the ruthless destruction by Chinese Communist soldiers of the ancient strongholds of Tantric Buddhism may have paved the way for a new day of opportunity for the gospel in the future. Even in Nigeria, the war served to demonstrate the bond of unity of Christian believers across tribal frontiers and provided the opportunity for acts of Christian reconciliation.

Nationalism

Wars in the past, such as the Second World War, have usually been the consequence of national pride and national self-interest. Nationalism itself – the longing to be free and independent, the desire for national self-expression and the right to enjoy the wealth and resources of one's own country all without foreign rule and exploitation – is a legitimate instinct. But when nationalism leads to hatred and violence at the expense of others or even of a nation's best interests, it becomes an instrument of evil forces.

Nationalism, smouldering between the two world wars and bursting into a flame after 1945, liberated the former colonial territories of European and American nations both in Asia and in Africa. The ensuing partition of India and Pakistan was accompanied by appalling massacres and followed by wars. In most countries a measure of disillusionment has followed independence. The expected prosperity did not come overnight, nor did peace. In Africa latent tribal rivalries flared into civil strife and in one new nation after another large numbers of people died. Democracy has largely gone by the board. 'Freedom' has been dearly bought. In Asian and African nations, corruption and inefficient government have played into the hands of extremists and prevented progress towards internal peace and prosperity. Nevertheless, in place of the old imperial empires, there are now 127 independent states represented in the United Nations – forty of them (nearly one third) in Africa. The Afro-Asian nations play a decisive role in the General Assembly.

Despite its follies, nationalism is a force of enormous strength, whether for good or evil, and needs to be understood. Communists have exploited it for their own ends. Is it possible or even right for the Christian church to harness nationalism for praiseworthy ends? Perhaps not. But certainly the Afro-Asian churches need to disengage from a Western culture, throw off purely foreign cultural accretions and become really indigenous to the soil of each country. Christianity is not a 'Western religion', and should never have been thought of as such.

National theologians are beginning to rethink biblical Christianity in their own cultural terms and to work out new church structures suited to their own cultures. While recognizing the possible danger of plunging the younger churches into the theological errors and the chaos of the first five centuries of the Christian era, it does seem necessary to produce an Asian theology at least which has taken into consideration the prevailing Hindu or Buddhist culture and climate of thought, in order to clarify the issues at stake and to emphasize the contrasts between natural and revealed religion. Such a study would not, of course, discard the theological achievements of Christianity in the past, but it would come to show the universal relevance of the Christian faith, not only in Western culture but in any culture. This study will provide an exciting sphere in which

Western Christians, with their Asian (and African) brethren, can think and pray together with a view to a more effective communication of the gospel and the creation of new patterns for church life and activity.

Resurgent religions

One significant feature of nationalism and its rejection of alien cultures imposed during the colonial period is the deliberate revival of old national cultures which are almost always centred in religion – 'a cultural nucleus'. Buddhism, for example, has been given a new name and status in Burma in order to displace the Christianity which once enjoyed special privilege under the British. In Thailand, too, Buddhism is equated with nationalism: 'If you cease to be a Buddhist you cease to be a Thai!' is the saying which Thai Christians have to live down. In Indonesia under the Dutch, Christianity was actually the state religion of the East Indies, but, when the Dutch left, Islam came back into its own. Hinduism, too, has enjoyed a restored prestige in India since independence. And even in animist Africa the traditional religious beliefs have been honoured in independence celebrations and fetish worship, once frowned upon, has been given a new dignity.

Thus Christianity no longer enjoys a special place of privilege in the world, but must contend with a resurgent Hinduism, which vehemently rejects the exclusive claims of Christ to be the revelation of God and the only way of access to God; a Buddhism whose highly ethical atheism challenges the superiority of Christ over Buddha; a militant Islam which specifically denies the deity of Christ and His death on the cross; and an animism which is no longer to be dismissed as 'primitive superstition', but claims the pride of place in African life denied to the 'white man's God'.

In the colonial era the great ethnic religions of the world were not taken seriously enough and only now is the church grappling with the philosophical and social challenge of these religions. However it is also true to say that revolution often loosens the iron chains of the old religions and makes people more open to new religious concepts. Christians must therefore take the old religions seriously, study them thoroughly and be able to demonstrate in what ways Christian thought differs from and is superior to the ancient philosophies. In the past the Christian approach has often been too negative in its attitude to other religions. What is needed is a deep understanding of their strength and weakness and, without any compromise, to be able to exalt Christ as the One in whom all wisdom is found and who is the world's only Saviour.

Racial tension

Race is a fundamental fact of life. We have the Arian or Caucasian race, the Slavic race, the Latin race, the Mongol race, the Semitic race and the Negro race. Akin to these larger groupings of mankind are the smaller groupings into thousands of different tribes or races. For sociological or economic reasons, races and tribes throughout the world commonly find themselves in dispute or friction through conflicting interests. Racialism is a harsh reality, almost as old as man.

In Africa, different colonial powers attempted different methods to solve the problems of European-African relationships. The French and Belgians tried cultural but not political integration. The Portuguese have practised complete racial integration while retaining political power in Portugal. The British favoured multi-racial societies to be prepared for eventual self-government. South Africa, where a 300-year-old European culture has come into conflict with the rights and interests of the Black Africans now living within the same national boundaries, was an entirely different problem. It is not surprising that the white South Africans resisted any suggestion of giving up their old established nation. The South African government has attempted the development of separate black and white cultures and plans eventually to create a number of separate and independent states based on separate African cultures. This is a serious attempt to solve a colossal and complex problem, but it has led to attitudes and injustices which have attracted world-wide criticism and could lead to a racial war if not corrected.

Elsewhere in Africa, however, old inter-tribal enmities, denied expression under colonial rule, have in the last decade been renewed in political rivalry and open warfare. Tribal hatreds die hard. Moreover Asians who have had their homes in

Africa for generations have also, for economic reasons, become the object of unjust discrimination by African states to the point of expulsion. The black racial feeling against former white masters and the fervent desire to see the Europeans all get out of Africa can be understood, but not justified, in the light of the continued need of African nations for European aid in the administration and development of their countries. Racialism is by no means a one-way evil; it is not simply white prejudice against dark-skinned people, but also dark-skinned prejudice against white, even dark against dark. Africans and Asians are just as guilty of racialism as their white fellowmen, even among those of their own colour and within a similar culture. Racialism is an outstanding expression of man's sinfulness and people of all races are equally guilty.

However, it is when, through the sins of earlier generations, as in the USA and the West Indies where Africans were introduced as slaves, or the historic events of recent history, as in the Middle East or in Great Britain, people of different races and contrasting cultures are thrown together unnaturally that the severest tensions are engendered. The presence of a black minority in North America, of the white minority in South Africa and of the immigrant minorities who during the last decade or so have flooded from several parts of the former 'British Empire' into Great Britain has created well-nigh insoluble problems. Manifest differences in race and culture – usually noble differences – are the common causes of incompatibility and racial prejudice, and these cannot be overcome by pretending the differences do not exist. It is difficult to foresee how Jews and Arabs in the Middle East, Indians and Pakistanis in the Indian sub-continent, Malays and Chinese in Malaysia, white and black Americans in North America, Ibos and Hausas in Nigeria, Southern Irish and Northern Irish in Ireland, blacks and whites in South Africa or Egyptian Arabs in North Sudan and black Africans in the South, can surmount racial and religious barriers in the interests of peace and brotherhood.

What is of supreme importance is that no-one should identify the Christian faith with any particular race, as if God were a European invention and Jesus a white man. The equation in South Africa of 'Christian civilization' with the white minority or with white people anywhere is the surest way to discredit Christianity in Africa generally. To imagine that God is on the side of the Jews against the Arabs would be a false reading of Scripture. Within the Christian church there are, according to Paul (Galatians 3:28), no racial or class distinctions, and while it must be left to education, public opinion and the sociologists to sort out the problems faced outside the church community, the church itself should set an example to the world of the kind of supra-national fellowship which exists within the church. For unless Christians can overcome racial prejudice the world is unlikely to be impressed by their professions of love and unity.

Secularism

Secularism is the belief or philosophy which attempts to explain life as a whole without reference to metaphysical or religious values. It is interested only in this world. This is not to say that secular man does not ask fundamental questions, but he tends to rule out in advance answers which have supernatural presuppositions.

Time magazine (January 1969) claimed that 'in the past three generations the everyday life of Western man has changed more than it did in the previous two thousand years'. The danger of this is seen in that throughout the world men have been taken captive by the materialistic spirit of the age and by the lure of the comforts and luxuries made possible by a modern technology. Thus modern secular man tends to live largely for his monthly salary or his weekly pay packet and for the pleasures and conveniences these can procure. In the West, if you are not in the well-paid executive class you try to increase your pay packet by the use of the strike weapon. Where the strike weapon is not an option, as in many under-privileged countries of the world, low-paid executives and workers alike indulge in corrupt financial practices in order to increase their material wealth. The unequal distribution of the world's wealth is one of the basic reasons for wars and revolutions, while poverty is found in the worst forms in the Third World.

The universal love of money and the absorption in the affairs of this world, whether in the West or in the East, make it increasingly difficult to convince secular man of moral and spiritual values, based on other-worldly presuppositions. Through materialism, as Paul says in 2 Corinthians 4:4, Satan blinds the mind and sears the conscience. Secularism provides a framework within which man need no longer think of God above or life beyond death.

Poverty and illiteracy
In bitter contrast to the crass materialism and growing affluence of the West a third of the world's population is said to suffer from malnutrition or even starvation. Mass hunger may be due to inadequate food supplies, or just to ignorance about normal dietary requirements, or both. For poverty and ignorance go hand in hand, and the dimensions of this twin problem are, even in the 1970s, enormous. Illiteracy is an enemy far from conquered, despite the immense efforts of the new independent nations to remove this stigma. United Nations figures suggest that 44 in every 100 people in the world are illiterate. In Asia the percentage is 65%. Illiteracy breeds ignorance and ignorance impedes progress. (See the diagram on page 20.)

Churches made up of illiterate Christians will not go far or earn wide esteem. Education, therefore, has been a major responsibility of the Christian church in under-developed countries and, even where the state is taking over the schools, Christian leaders still enjoy great opportunities. Education will promote progress and progress will ultimately increase economic strength, both within and without the churches.

It is important, however, in this connection not to confuse simplicity with poverty. Tribes in some parts of the world live a very simple, primitive existence. But the array of thick silver neckbands and silver or gold ornaments worn by both men and women, as in Thailand, show that they are not everywhere poor. The tribes people of the Philippines at times have adequate supplies of rice and so do not starve, but their ignorance of dietary laws does result in very general vitamin deficiency and malnutrition, often mistakenly called starvation.

When the Christian church is planted among simple people it is important not to assume the necessity for a church to possess Western style buildings and elaborate church organization.

No church is so poor that, if trained in Christian stewardship, it cannot develop its life, ministry and witness within the simplicity of its own setting. There is a positive approach to the economic environment of most churches without the use of traditional and pauperizing Western subsidies and aids.

The New Left

In a secular world torn by civil war, threatened with nuclear destruction, plagued by racial tension and haunted by either the spectre of a world-wide famine or an ecological disaster, it is not surprising if an idealist younger generation is bitterly critical of a society marred, as they see it, by the follies of an older generation. For our advanced technology has opened up the possibilities of something far better. Some opt out of an 'artificial' society altogether by way of protest and may form new and strange communities of hippies, yippies or whatever the latest name for them may be, to experiment with new ways of community living. Unfortunately, drugs are usually associated with this way of life and the sole ethic is that of 'love' – chiefly in the erotic sense of the word. 'You've gotta believe in love!' says the pop song. But these are in the minority. Others, not content just to opt out of society, want desperately to change it fundamentally. They are in revolt against the dehumanizing tendencies of our present-day world, against a computerized society and the loneliness of mass man. These new revolutionaries are against what they regard as *bourgeois* standards of conduct and living. They also tend to be against authority, against war, against racialism. Many are genuinely concerned about poverty and social justice and therefore they want to change the structures of society which has produced so many evils and to build something new in its place.

A feature of this movement is the student unrest which has exploded into violence all over the world, but especially in Japan. In Latin America, the younger generation, especially the student class, are in revolt against the traditional aristocratic style of government there and the gross economic inequality and social injustice which has prevailed for so long. The successful revolution in Cuba made Fidel Castro a continental hero. Now South America has its first Marxist state in Chile where

Fidel Castro received a rapturous welcome in late 1971. Christians share the deep desire for social change but, while rejecting the Marxist hypothesis, they are hard put to it to find an alternative radical movement to support. Most of the New Left accept the Marxist analysis of society but are not necessarily Communists. Many are anarchists who are determined to destroy the present structures but have little idea what to erect in their place. They often overlook the fact that all revolutions, while successful in removing some evils, have also given birth to new and equally great evils. Social change does not necessarily mean change for the better. Nevertheless under these new revolutionary stresses society in every continent shows signs of steady disintegration.

At the All India Congress on Evangelism in 1969 the following statement was issued: 'We are conscious that we live in revolutionary times manifested in political instability, social and industrial unrest, moral bankruptcy, communal riots and youth revolts.' True of India, these words are almost equally true of the world as a whole. John Mackay of Princeton University rightly says, 'Revolution is a sacred word for millions of people around the globe. The sanctity of revolution is steadily growing. Many concerned people everywhere are convinced that revolutionary changes should take place in man's life and relationships by non-violent and constitutional procedures. Increasing numbers of people are convinced that the changes so desperately needed in the social and political structures can only be brought about by methods which make violence inevitable. This new philosophy of violence is linked with racialism and nationalism and the influence of Marxist theology.' But as President Kennedy once said, 'Those who make peaceful revolution impossible will make violent revolution inevitable.' Christians everywhere should be foremost among those who are seeking to promote a peaceful revolution.

Humanism
What can be done about a situation which seems to deteriorate with every year that passes? Both Humanists and Communists tend to be optimists because they base their convictions on an evolutionary theory which teaches inevitable progress towards

an ultimately good society. Humanists from Confucius to Huxley have had a naive faith in the innate goodness of human nature and its ability, given time and education, to surmount all obstacles and to achieve a just and dignified society in which man can enjoy happiness and fulfilment.

Communism

Karl Marx, on the other hand, was more incisive in his analysis of the human dilemma. He saw man as the victim of his own environment. Evil and suffering therefore originate in the imperfect ordering of society, economically speaking. Thus, if society can be changed, human nature can also be changed and Huxley's 'brave new world' then becomes a possibility, indeed a certainty. Marx did not believe in gradual and peaceful change, but insisted on violent revolution which he believed could alone bring about the essential reversal of the classes, capitalist and proletariat, and transfer to the proletariat power to build a socialist society. This materialist and socialist dream has for over fifty years held out to millions of under-privileged human beings the hope of a just and peaceful world. Violent and bloody revolutions have taken place in many countries of the world. Some have failed or run out of steam. Others are plotted. The majority of Communists in non-Communist lands have little idea what Communists really believe or what a terrible and violent thing a Communist revolution really is. They mistakenly tend to think of Communism as nothing more than a vital and virile form of enlightened socialism.

Despite a growing disillusionment with orthodox Communism, its traditional dogmatism and manifest short-comings, world revolution is still the openly-declared aim of the true Communist. Nothing has changed here. If Russia, the formerly accepted leader of the world revolution, has faltered in this course in favour of 'peaceful co-existence' between the two systems, China, under Chairman Mao, has not. China is definitely the present spearhead of the world revolution and is actively encouraging 'wars of liberation' wherever possible. Chinese moral and material support lies behind the long-drawn-out war in Vietnam. Indian Maoists are actively working for power in that continent, while China threatens the entire northern border of India. 'Africa is ripe for revolution,' said Chou En-Lai a few years ago, and ever since Maoist Chinese have been pouring into Tanzania and Zambia, to Guinea and Ghana. They are training the Freedom Fighters as they trained the murderous Simbas in the Congo. Their hand is seen in almost every subversive activity and they have been behind some, at least, of the many *coups d'état*. Cuba too probably owes more to Peking than to Moscow and the Latin American revolutionary heroes are no longer Marx and Lenin but Mao, Marcuse and Che Guevara. All over the world, in London as well as Manila, groups of young revolutionaries proudly call themselves Maoists rather than Marxists.

What is the difference? For one thing the Mao-led revolution was not an orthodox Marxist revolution by the industrialist working-class, but one in which the peasants played a leading role. Nor does Mao consider the revolution to be a once-for-all affair; there must be 'permanent revolution' renewed in each generation, as demonstrated by the Red Guards in the Great Proletarian Cultural Revolution of 1966–69. Thirdly, Mao took the Western philosophical system of Marx and gave it an oriental philosophical basis. He even injected into it something of Confucian ethics and Buddhist mysticism. But the cult of Mao and the exaltation of his thoughts enshrined in the *Little Red Book* of quotations from Mao's speeches display many of the features of religious revivalism. Mao Tse-tung is passionately revered as the great leader who, by the power of his spoken and written wisdom, has brought China from weakness to strength. Popular songs exalt Mao as China's 'great red sun'. The *Little Red Book* is carried on the person by every Chinese, and read, studied, memorized and applied as by Christians with their Bible. Popular fervour reaches white heat whenever the Chairman appears in public.

Christian answer

With the divine revelation, the Word of God, in hand, the Christian, of all people, ought to be able to speak to the world in every age with complete authority. The laws of God and the teachings of Christ and the apostles are an all-sufficient guide to man in his search for a personal and social ethic. The ultimate issue is God or Mammon? Christ or Caesar? The tragedy is that man in his revolt against God refuses to consider God's revelation seriously. Even Christians need to be instructed in the biblical principles of social and political involvement in the society of which they are a part, as well as in the doctrines of salvation. A Christian must really care about social inequalities and a missionary cannot afford to perpetuate them in his own standard of living and attitudes to the people around him.

But supremely in the gospel of Christ's death and resurrection there is a way provided to reconcile man to God. The true gospel is actually more revolutionary than any other ideology and contains the dynamic man needs to change human nature and so to revolutionize society. Love is not the modern discovery of the folk and pop song-writers. After all it was Christ, not the modern social drop-outs, who, two thousand years ago, summed up the essential ethic as 'love is all' – love for God and love for men. The church is the custodian of this message – the answer of God to the plight of man. Paul also faced a disintegrating society which he describes in Romans 1. He had become convinced that the answer was the gospel, the dynamite or power of God, of which he was proud to be a messenger.

But what does the church today do about it? What do you and I do about it? Either we hoard the message selfishly for ourselves without any deep conviction that this is the good news essential for all mankind. Or our theologians call the gospel itself in question and undermine the faith of Christians in its validity for themselves, much less for others. Or our Christian secularists drain the gospel of its essence and then act as if adding their voice of protest against racialism in South Africa or social conditions in Notting Hill was all that mattered. Or the sects pervert the gospel in a score of different ways, so that the church no longer speaks with one voice and spreads confusion as to what the gospel really is. Or Christians regard the taking of the gospel to others as an optional and extravagant extra which the church cannot afford. Some seem to see the preservation of old and historic church buildings as having priority over the church's task of evangelism. Others will parrot the old slogan 'Charity begins at home', i.e. with the needs of our own people; they scarcely stop to think why it must be 'me first' or that, while charity may begin at home, it can never end there. One African Christian leader wryly comments that the only 'closed doors' in the world are those in the minds of Western Christians whose present apathy makes them coolly indifferent to God's world-wide programme for mankind as a whole.

The church in the world is at war. But defeat has never been in question. John describes Christ as the One who goes forth 'conquering and to conquer' (Revelation 6:2). One day the kingdoms of this world are to become the Kingdom of our Lord and of His Christ (Revelation 11:15). Until then we must continue to declare Christ's Lordship wherever He is not known and acknowledged and so, together with all the redeemed multitudes, prepare the way for His coming.

BIBLIOGRAPHY
Missions in Crisis by Eric S. Fife and Arthur F. Glasser (Inter-Varsity Press, 1962).
Is Revolution Change? edited by Brian Griffiths (Inter-Varsity Press, 1972).
Christianity and Comparative Religion by J. N. D. Anderson (Tyndale Press, 1970).

Problems to ponder
Reaching African students in South Africa

Higher education
Each of the five major racial groups in South Africa has its own universities and colleges: 1. African; 2. Afrikaner; 3. Coloured (mixed race); 4. Indian; 5. English speaking (this includes Jewish and Chinese students in some universities).

'African' is a term covering at least eight different language groups, each with a self-conscious, cultural identity. Africans can also be divided into 'rural' and 'urban' Africans. Africans, of course, compose the great majority of the national population, but their universities and colleges, though expanding rapidly, are fewer in proportion and often in remote situations.

Rural African students – their situation

These usually come from homes where there is a strong emphasis on kinship and solidarity, reinforced by reverence for ancestors, a deep respect for taboos and the practice of witchcraft. But their secondary education has probably been in mission-type boarding schools with a tradition of narrowly Protestant Christianity and a middle-class imprint largely unrelated to the home and family situation. There is frequently, therefore, a dichotomy between school and family. While they sing Christian choruses beautifully, few have been taught to relate doctrine to ethics and to the cultural conservatism of their rural environment. The decreasing influence of missions in education is resulting in a corresponding ignorance of supernatural Christianity.

Case 1

Miriam wanted to know what she, as a Christian, should do about her family who were consulting the witch doctor. Should she, out of respect, go along with her parents or stand out against them? If so, how should she explain her position? Conversation revealed that Miriam had not had much teaching on what a Christian may or may not do in practice and little on Christ's victory over Satanic forces and how to pray for others to be released from those powers.

Miriam was also troubled – like other girls – about the practice in rural areas of parentally-arranged marriages and the problem of 'lobola' or dowry. Indeed, the whole subject of marriage and its purpose, the body and its functions as taught in Scripture and the role of the Holy Spirit were areas where teaching was desperately needed. How does the Holy Spirit in the Christian relate to the cultural conservatism of the rural situation?

Problem. What help would you have given in this case? (Discuss.)

Urban African students – their situation

These have come from either mission boarding schools or government schools. Most are removed by one or two generations from a 'Christian' background. The girls include fewer outright agnostics than the men, who tend to be more militantly unbelieving. Urban students retain basically conservative African attitudes, but without the group ethos and explicit religious taboos of the rural African, though the taboo complex remains. In a European environment, they must fend for themselves as individuals; the old structure of parental authority has disintegrated in a situation in which the father is away from home earning his living, while the mother and grandmother try to make ends meet. This results, sometimes, in resort to crime to obtain money and to sexual laxity. In fact, urban students live in a corrupt society and tend to regard Christianity as the religion of the European and merely a feature of Western civilization. They have not been confronted with the gospel as a contemporary faith relevant to their urban situation and social and political aspirations – particularly those connected with African consciousness and 'black power'. They often see being a Christian as a position opposed to this new African identity and therefore have no wish to become Christian.

Problem. How would you counsel a student with these very real problems? (Discuss first before reading further.)

Teaching is needed about God's plan for mankind in unity and diversity (*cf.* Acts 17:26) and the attitude of Jesus Christ to such problems and what it means to be inter-dependent in the family of God.

Case 2

Mary was a Christian, but became involved in immorality, had a breakdown and went into a mental hospital. After recovering, she wanted to know how to cope with her situation and whether she should tell her new Christian boy friend about her past experience. The teaching of 1 Corinthians was absolutely relevant.

Case 3

William had a problem about suffering and social injustice. He said he could not believe in a God who permitted such things. It took a long time to work through the usual cultural stereotypes before he saw man's need and sin as a human being – that sin which causes anti-social behaviour. Only then could

William see the relevance of Christ's reconciling work and the reality of a visible future salvation when the present defaced image of God in man will be replaced by a new humanity in Christ which will retain both unity and diversity (*cf*. Revelation 7:9). The truth which eventually cleared the mental fog was that of Christ as the One who identified Himself with suffering humanity and Himself suffered creatively and who is now our Contemporary. The ultimate challenge was to let God cleanse us first before we become involved in action to help solve the current social and racial problems.

4
How to win the world – back to first principles

Misunderstandings

Lord Montgomery's biting criticism has often been quoted: 'The British Army went into World War II admirably equipped and organized to fight the 1914 War and with the wrong officers at the top.' These words are very relevant to the subject of this chapter.

'The world scene is moving at an increasingly rapid pace. Mission concepts that were valid 20 years ago may not be useful today. Mission policies designed for the steamship era seem strangely anachronistic in a jet age' (Edward Dayton in *World Vision*, June 1970). Much muddled thinking even among missionaries and out-moded concepts of what missionary work is among the general public still persists alarmingly. Executive mission councils, too often made up of men who have no experience of work overseas, tend to be conservative in their thinking and often chiefly concerned apparently to preserve the *status quo*. So how can their Christian supporters be expected to know the score?

To the general public 'missionaries' are nothing better than well-meaning do-gooders who, wearing pith helmets and ankle-length skirts, presumptuously try to induce 'primitive' people to accept an alien Western religion by offers of material gain and by running bush hospitals for the sick or 'old dame schools' for the illiterate. Is this a true picture or a caricature? It is surely a fact that education and medicine have often been the twin foci of traditional missionary work. The public commonly thinks of missionaries as either doctors, nurses or teachers, or possibly parsons! But it is time to state quite unequivocally that education and medicine are in themselves activities only secondary to the main task of the church – that of preaching Christ and of bringing together and teaching those who respond by trusting Him. In technical terms, church planting and church growth should be the primary concern of missionaries.

The persisting image of the missionary is of someone who lives and works in a rural area and among 'primitive people' with the object of persuading them to accept some of the dubious advantages of Western civilization. And unfortunately much of the presentation to the churches and the public in Great Britain, USA or Australasia merely perpetuates the image. What church people are told, simply because it is what they want most to hear, often has little direct bearing on the real action in the campaign for the evangelization of the world. It is a sad reflection on human nature that what people want to read about in their daily papers or in missionary literature is the sensational and dramatic. The solid, basic, humdrum work of the faithful church-planting missionary seldom provides the material for a popular best-seller. It is well-known that certain charities and certain forms of mission attract money in very large amounts, though they usually have little to do with the primary function of the church. The all-important and primary work of 'church planting' and 'church growth' is certainly not a fund-raiser.

However, much hard thinking on the subject by scholars, theologians and missionaries has been done in recent decades. Many thoughtful and scholarly books have been written and some radically-thinking missionary statesmen – or Monty's modern generals – have emerged. Refreshing winds are blowing through the musty atmosphere of many a mission board room and field councils are embarking on imaginative, even revolutionary, new experiments. But the real problem is how to enthuse the church at large about the basic principles and the high strategy of mission and how to persuade society leaders, missionaries and their supporters to jettison old cargoes and load up with new ones. Nevertheless a solution must be found.

'Strategy' is a military term, meaning 'the art of war' or 'generalship'. In waging war the first duty of the High Command is clearly to define both its objectives and the means by which those objectives can be reached. Business and industry have long recognized the importance of goals – objectives against which performance can be measured. Without them organizations get bogged down in meaningless motion. From the start, Christianity operated with a clearly-defined goal, given in Acts 1:8 – to be witnesses for Christ to the end of the earth, and in Matthew 28:18, 19 to go and make disciples of all nations (*cf.* also Mark 16:15, 16; Luke 24:47; John 20: 21–23).

But it is only when subsidary goals are brought in line with the ultimate goal that Christian energy will be spent in the right direction. It is therefore not sufficient to say, as they did in 1910, that our objective is 'The evangelization of the world in this generation'. That may be a true aim and, as a vague generalization, it is readily understood, but it is in defining the means to attain that objective that there has been so much mistaken, inadequate or muddled thinking.

In the last century, Christians in the West considered it to be their responsibility to go to earth's remotest bounds to proclaim the name of Jesus Christ and to win souls for the Kingdom. And go they did, at great cost in sacrifice, hardship and loss of life. The emphasis was on 'winning souls'. But there were never nearly enough volunteers to ensure that the whole world could be reached by foreign missionaries with the gospel in one generation; and despite much expenditure of life and wealth the objective was never attained, because the tactics used were wrong. There was too little emphasis on the New Testament role and function of the church. Some mission leaders still think of world evangelization in terms of recruiting larger and larger numbers of British or American missionaries to go overseas to swell the ranks of evangelists. There are even people who actually assess the relative success of missionary societies by the number of baptisms or conversions they can respectively record each year – a criterion which has little relation to the policies and practices of the apostles in the New Testament.

The number of converts was less important initially than the formation of strong local church groups.

Paul's initial objective was, no doubt, the 'winning of souls', but only as the first step. More important to the apostles was the next step – the planting of churches. The book of Acts is the textbook in this respect as well as a unique history of early church practice. Evangelism was never thought of as an end in itself, but only the means to an end. The churches planted in each locality were then taught to become themselves the bases for further evangelism and spontaneous expansion. The responsibility for local evangelism passed at an early stage from the apostle to the local church (cf. 1 Thessalonians 1:8). It ceased to be the responsibility of the apostle (or the 'foreign missionary'). New Testament thought and activity are completely church-centred. There is extensive teaching in the Epistles about the church in terms of a body or living organism, with many individual members (cf. Romans 12:4,5; 1 Corinthians 12:12; Ephesians 4:1–16), or of a building to which individual bricks are continually being added (1 Peter 2:4,5). The Epistles are all addressed to local churches or church leaders. Any activity therefore which is merely mission-centred or pure individualism and not church-centred cannot be called New Testament activity.

No-one can deny that we live in a period of rapid change which is deeply affecting the role of the church and its outreach in the world today. But nothing can alter the plainly revealed, inviolable purpose of God for the evangelization of the world. The local church is still, as it always has been, the strategic factor in the carrying out of God's plan – God's secret weapon. As Sir Kenneth Grubb says: 'A mission which does not lead to a church has usually failed to fulfil its purpose; a church which does not lead to a mission has usually lost its vision.'

Biblical principles

In the Old Testament it is clear that God's purposes for the pagan world were to be fulfilled through Israel – Araham's seed in whom *all* the nations of the world were to be blessed (Genesis 26:4, AV; Psalm 67:1,2; Isaiah 49:6). But Israel

completely failed God in that responsibility because of her con
promise, ignorance and disobedience. Finally, God sent His
Son, the Seed, to become, through His church, a light to lighten
the nations and His salvation before the face of *all peoples*
(Luke 2:29–32). Where Israel failed, Christ through the
church, His Body, was to succeed, as Peter writes, 'You are a
chosen race ... that you may declare the wonderful deeds of
him who called you out of darkness into his marvellous light'
(1 Peter 2:9). Filled with the Holy Spirit, the early church
was a missionary church with a world-wide mission. But all
too soon the conservative elements tried to apply the brakes
and to confine the gospel to the Jews. It took the dramatic conversion of the apostle Paul and a remarkable vision to a pre-
judiced apostle Peter to release the flood-gates and set in motion
the multiplication of churches in ever-widening circles throughout the world.

The church universal is made up, not so much of single individuals as of numerous local churches the world over – the
living, reproducing cells of the whole living church organism.
The individual cannot isolate himself from the life of the local
church if he is to be a fully functioning Christian. The church's
primary duty, therefore, quite contrary to much current practice, is to evangelize the world by multiplying itself in tens of
thousands of local churches so situated that the entire population of the world is brought within sound of the gospel; not
through thousands of foreign missionaries but through thousands of congregations of people proclaiming that gospel in the
language of their own country, region or tribe. Like the church
in Thessalonica, the church, not Paul the missionary, is to be
the sounding board for the gospel (1 Thessalonians 1:8, J. B.
Phillips). That is the unchanging over-all strategic concept and
it has been well summarized in the slogan: 'A church in every
community and *thereby* the gospel to every creature.' That is
how the gospel spread historically in the days of the early church
and that is how it is spreading today where the New Testament
pattern is followed. Note the slogan does not say 'The gospel
to every creature and thereby a church in every community';
that would be to put the cart before the horse. Unless the objective of planting a church in every community is kept clearly

in focus, frustrating defeat will be inevitable; for to substitute plans of our own in place of God's plan will lead to disaster. It is essential, therefore, to evaluate every 'missionary' activity by the extent to which it contributes to this primary objective. Otherwise Christian workers will continue to get bogged down in purely secondary pursuits which are not necessarily contributing to the main aim. God's strategic unit, let us repeat, is the local church.

The New Testament emphasis on the local church as the geographical focus of God's strategic plan was clearly not designed to lead to the proliferation of totally independent and doctrinally discordant churches. Each was to recognize its membership within and oneness with a larger whole, the worldwide church of Jesus Christ, and to accept the absolute authority of Holy Scripture in matters of doctrine and life. The fact that today, in the Third World, acute rivalry exists between the many churches and denominations founded by Western missionaries, and that newly planted or break-away churches often adopt new and curious variations of the New Testament church, does not invalidate the basic principle or cast reflection on God's originally revealed strategic plan. The confusion which exists is a measure of the Enemy's intense hostility to the building of the city of God. 'I will build my church, and the powers of death shall not prevail against it' (Matthew 16:18). Donald MacGavran writes: 'The Christian Church stands at the beginning of her mission. The minor church growth of the nineteenth and twentieth centuries is only the prologue. The great turnings to Christ and the mighty multiplication of His Church lie ahead. The era of church planting has only begun. In the midst of these revolutionary movements, let us press forward, turning the world upside down and leading multitudes everywhere to Christ.'

Military strategy

Once the High Command has clarified the military objectives and the over-all strategy, it then entrusts the carrying out of that strategy to the area staffs, the commanding officers, and the officers on the field. It should by now be plain that the field strategy of a mission agency can never adequately be determined by remote mission councils or boards in London or Washington. The evangelistic and church-planting activities of the apostles were never controlled from Jerusalem. Field councils are the equivalent of the area COs and their staff officers and they must be given full authority for field administration, just as the apostle Paul and his team exercised their authority on the spot. For them the guiding principles must be, as in war, an offensive, positive spirit which seeks to keep the initiative; mobility in contrast to the static 'mission station' mentality together with flexibility and the element of surprise. The follow-up of initial victories is absolutely vital, for the world is littered with the relics of initial victories which were not exploited. Paul was always revisiting the churches he had planted (Acts 15:36) or writing letters to them to correct, encourage and instruct them in their corporate life.

Attention needs also to be paid to the economic use of available manpower and resources with constant reference to priorities; there is undoubtedly far too much overlapping and a wasteful use of missionary personnel. Finally, the entire action must be co-ordinated as far as possible to achieve the common objectives. Much more consultation and closer co-operation between the churches everywhere and the missions which serve them are desirable. Many things like theological and Bible colleges, educational establishments, medical facilities, radio and literature projects, can all be done better by co-operation than in isolation and independency.

While the practice of these strategic or tactical principles can be clearly traced in the Acts and in the early history of the church, it is also possible to observe their subsequent neglect by a church which has lost its vision. It is now time for the church once again to study, understand and apply these basic principles in the changed and changing world situation of the 1970s.

Paul's methods

Incontestably the four stages in Paul's strategy were: 1. Evangelism – the preaching and the proclamation of the Person, the death and the resurrection of Christ and the forgiveness of sins and eternal life for those who would repent and believe

(Romans 1:16; 1 Corinthians 15:3,4). 2. The gathering together of those believers into a corporate, organized fellowship
– a local microcosm of the Body of Christ. 3. The systematic
instruction of the believers in discipleship, the training for
leadership and the proper exercise of all the gifts of the Spirit
(Acts 19:9,10). 4. The emphasis on the responsibility of the
local church to pass on the truth it had received to all within
its own radius of influence and beyond (Acts 19:10; 1 Thessalonians 1:8). Clearly Paul established churches, not 'mission
stations'. He and the colleagues in his team regarded themselves as but temporary instruments for evangelizing, church-
planting and teaching. They avoided becoming the focus of the
work and passed on as soon as possible, leaving churches dependent, not on them, but on God the Holy Spirit for their
survival and proper function.

Traditional pattern
During the past 150 years the educational and medical needs
in many parts of the world have admittedly been very great.
And so missionary societies have often allocated most of their
manpower and financial resources to schools and hospitals.
These institutions necessitated a complex of buildings including a church which, with the several missionary residences and
residences for native staff, constituted the typical 'mission station'. This phenomenon was essentially foreign in character and
missionary-centred. Mission stations often developed into
Christian communities or ghettoes in which the native Christian became largely isolated from the stream of national life.
Both in India and Africa they were a pale reflection of the
colonial system. The missionary was a kind of second-class civil
servant and enjoyed much of the prestige and status of the ruling power.
    When in the forties imperialism and colonialism became fin-
ally discredited and the European rulers left, turning over their
responsibilities and property to the nationals, the missionaries
on their 'compounds' found themselves in an embarrassing and
anachronistic situation. Some, no doubt, were so used to the
old ways and so insensitive to the radical changes taking place
around them that they were hardly aware of the 'mission

station' anomaly and the distaste with which non-Christians regarded these alien phenomena. This old-fashioned hand-me-down is being discarded nearly everywhere. The very terminology of 'mission station' and 'mission field' is recognized as the vocabulary of a past age. But the hang-over of the colonial mentality has yet to be deliberately and finally rejected. If the missionary is to decrease as national leadership increases, he should rejoice.

But in spite of missions having been excusably children of this age and having too often reproduced Western patterns of church life and activity they did succeed in planting the cross throughout the world. Today the existence of a world-wide church is a fact for which God must be praised.

Unfinished task

Does this, then, suggest that the missionary task of the church is done? By no means! It has already been stated that the dimension of the task is not merely to the end of the earth but also to the end of the age. The task will only then be complete and until that moment it must be pursued with all the church's energies. Primary evangelism and the planting of churches is only Stage One in world evangelization. The second stage is to ensure that, working out from every church base, the entire population of the world will be reached with the gospel. It cannot be repeated too often that, despite the present realization of a universal church, the vast majority of the world's present population is still unevangelized. Huge pockets of population remain unreached; whole segments of society do not know Christ; each new generation needs a new approach. Some areas are geographically remote from any local church. So the church cannot afford to lose its evangelizing momentum and its burning desire to bring the gospel to the ears of every creature.

To illustrate the present situation we may say that we now need, not a map covered with dots to represent 'mission stations', but a map covered with arrows to indicate movement and planned direction in evangelism. 'The day of the pioneer in his pith helmet in past. We can do without the helmet and the little tin god mentality that goes with it. The eclipsing of the image gives us no pangs of regret. But to see that which was the impetus for world-wide witness caricatured and sneered at is a different matter. Bury the pith helmets – but please, not the spirit that fired the men that wore them l' (Arthur Mathews, 'Pioneer Equivalents in the Seventies' in *East Asia Millions* (USA), November 1970).

A shared task

But now, note an all-important change of emphasis. The evangelistic task must be seen today as the task of the whole church throughout the world, and therefore to be shared by every local church that makes up that whole; African, Latin American, Asian, French and Russian churches, just as much as American or British churches. 'It is quite time we stopped identifying church denominations, however large or "catholic", with the universal Body of Christ or its local manifestations. To Christians in the Third World, even the older denominations, despite their longer history and higher prestige, often appear as highly sectarian bodies whose historical peculiarities have far less to commend them than Europeans and North Americans presume to believe. For the historic denominations to look over their fences and call the newer denominations "sects" is a rather fantastic piece of presumption. All of our denominations are "sects"; they are cuttings or sections of the Christian community.' So writes Paul S. Rees in *World Vision* (March 1960).

If God's strategic unit is the local church, each local church must become an effective fighting unit in the war, engaged in aggressive evangelism, using methods suited to the culture of its own environment. Clearly, the success of this over-all strategy depends on the effectiveness of each unit, that is each local church. God's purpose will fail, either if there are not enough local churches in the world to reach the unreached millions, or if the local church is not functioning properly. This basic plan of action, as unchanging as the Word of God itself, should be at the head of the agenda of every council of missionaries.

An effective local church

To be effective in war an army needs to be thoroughly trained down to the smallest unit. It is not enough for any local church to have a good pastor or minister in order to function properly.

There can be no pew-sitters. The model church is one in which the entire membership is thoroughly grounded in the Word of God. Parents are taught how to teach their own children. The children are taught systematically, both at home and in graded Sunday Schools. Sunday School teachers are trained to teach effectively. Adolescents are taught regular methods of personal devotion and brought into lively youth fellowships where all life's problems are faced and discussed in the light of the Bible. Youth leaders and Bible class leaders are adequately trained for the task. Adults can never afford to stop learning and so are involved in a continuous teaching and learning ministry under competent leaders. Deacons and elders are ideally men and women of spiritual stature emerging from the congregation.

The minister clearly needs to be a well-trained experienced leader of men, a man with a thorough doctrinal and theological training and full acquaintance with current problems in the society around. It is for him to provide an all-round teaching and inspirational ministry strictly relevant to the everyday needs of his congregation and their many social involvements. He must also encourage the exercise of all the gifts of the Spirit to the congregation, co-ordinate their activities and above all keep the church constantly aware of its *raison d'être*; that is, not to be merely a warm joyful fellowship (it should be that!) but to witness faithfully and persistently to the truth of the gospel among neighbours, business associates, school and college associates and the entire local populace All this must be included in a clear vision of the church's share in total world evangelization. The local church work must always be seen in the context of the world-wide church. Happy the church in England, Nigeria, the Philippines, Japan or Bolivia that has members serving abroad, thus involving it directly in the world-wide work of the church.

To sum up the priorities; we must first establish productive patterns of church life; second, maintain consistent Bible teaching programmes; third, engage in church-based evangelistic outreach; and fourth, provide leadership training for every aspect of church life. John Wesley's theological 'professors' were, in effect, church-planters who started 'classes' and trained class leaders. The Communists borrowed his methods and cell struc-

tures and harnessed them to the conversion of the world. The
New Testament church was a growing, multiplying church.
Why should we expect anything less today?

International Fellowships

Already pan-confessional movements, Anglican, Lutheran
Methodist, *etc*. are, for better or for worse, recognizable in every
continent. But new patterns of internationalism are developing
quite apart from these old 'denominational' affiliations. New
groupings are taking place unrelated to the ecumenical movement. The desire for a true 'unity of the Spirit' is not confined to
the confessional churches or to church union; supra-national
teams of co-workers are becoming increasingly common in
every continent. There are people of many nationalities on the
staffs of Bible and theological colleges, in schools and hospitals
and even within the local churches. It can already be seen that
in Christ there is neither Jew nor Greek, neither bond nor free,
neither male nor female. Racial and class distinctions or distinctions on the ground of sex disappear. 'Missionaries' will not
in future be, as hitherto, members of a white foreign legion so
much as members of a world-wide Christian fellowship in
which all races are represented. A few missionary societies are
in a small degree inter-racial and supra-national. But a small
Asian or Latin American membership in a large Western missionary society faces serious problems. There is a schizophrenic
dilemma: 'Do I belong to the Asian community, the Latin community or to the foreign missionary community? Where is my
real affinity? Where is my prior loyalty?' In the final analysis,
the Asian or Latin American, largely supported as he is from
alien sources, owes extra-territorial loyalties to a society heavily
dominated by Westerners, as Dennis Clark has pointed out.
And in the present climate of opinion in the Third World the
position of such a national eventually becomes untenable. Some
alternative must be found. It could possibly be found in autonomous 'associate' missions on a continental basis.

Gift of teachers

If it is the prime function of every local church to evangelize,
then what is the proper function of the ex-patriate from Japan

or Canada who desires to identify himself with a local church? This will clearly depend on the gifts God has given him and which will be recognized and put to use in association with all the other members of the church. Generally speaking, Christians from the West have had greater advantages in education and Bible knowledge and their main contribution will therefore be to teach the Word of God at every level of need and to train others to teach within the framework of a Christian education for every Christian. (Is the task of the modern missionary beginning to gain clear definition?)

Training leaders
No church will be strong without enlightened, spiritual leadership. It may be that in a possible Communist takeover, as in China, or a nationalist purge of all foreigners, as in Burma, no church will even survive without sturdy Spirit-filled leaders. The gift of leadership may be expected to emerge within the life of every healthy local church. But this gift also needs to be developed and its possessor fully trained. Bible schools and theological colleges will undoubtedly multiply in the coming years to meet the growing need of the growing churches and, with that, theologically trained men and women must also be multiplied. Thus a tremendous challenge confronts Western theologians, for there is a growing desire on the part of Afro-Asians and Latin Americans to re-formulate theology so as to make it relevant to the culture and needs of each country. In this task East and West will work together and the theological qualifications of Westerners will need to be matched by a deep sensitivity, sympathy and insight.

But theological and Bible colleges are already proving insufficient to meet the demands for more and more good lay leadership. To this end the extension of formal theological training to the leading laymen of the churches is a prospect with enormous promise. 'Extension theological education is the most significant development in theological education in the twentieth century,' one American missionary leader has said. The World Evangelical Fellowship has set up Theological Assistance Programme to help meet the need for theologically equipped national leaders in the Third World.

Wherever these biblical emphases on the mobilization of the whole church for evangelism and the careful instruction of every church member in effective witness have been made, extraordinary movements of church growth have resulted, especially in recent decades.

Kenneth Strachan of Latin America conceived the movement known as Evangelism-in-Depth, which enshrined just these principles – getting all the churches into motion to evangelize the total community. His main thesis was: 'The growth of any movement is in direct proportion to the success of that movement in mobilizing its total membership in the constant propagation of its beliefs.' In one country after another in Central and South America a profound impact has been made on entire nations by the application of this principle and the churches have added tens of thousands to their membership, although, for want of edequate 'follow-up' and other reasons, there has been considerable wastage.

These principles were later adopted and adapted to the Nigerian setting under the name of 'New Life for All'. In the three years following, the churches of Northern Nigeria doubled their membership and the movement continues to grow. The same principles are being taught and applied in Zaire under the name 'Christ for the Zaire' and also in South Africa by the 'New Life for All' movement. In fact, saturation evangelism programmes are in progress in twenty-seven African states south of the Sahara.

An office of Evangelism-in-Depth has been set up in Singapore and principles put into operation in Latin America and Africa are being studied throughout Asia with a view to adapting their use to Asian conditions. Already there has been a successful 'saturation evangelism' campaign in Shikoku, one of the four largest islands of Japan.

In Pasadena, California, a Church Growth Institute is making a scientific study of the applications of biblical principles to particular situations and is trying to discover the divine laws of church growth, not overlooking economic and sociological factors. 'People movements' of the past have been investigated and the lessons they teach have been learned, with a view to harnessing present-day movements, like those in Indonesia and Chile, for the growth and enrichment of the whole church of Christ.

Donald MacGavran, director of the Church Growth Institute, has this to say: 'The disproportionate and malign influence which India, Ceylon, China and other resistant nations have had on Christian mission must now be ended. The defeatism, pessimism and hopelessness which decades of fruitless missionary labours have caused must no longer cast a shadow across the responsive nations of the world. Modes of missions which seem correct in populations rejecting the Gospel must not be used among those welcoming it. The Church must focus her eyes on Brazil, Africa, Chile and Indonesia and other lands where tremendous and sound growth of the Church is as normal as it was in the New Testament times and continually try out in resistant and semi-resistant segments of society methods of discipling proved effective in responsive countries.'

United action

Some might be tempted to think that the administrative and strategic confusion of the past could be ended if a mission high command had authority to enforce on all missions the principles and strategy outlined in this chapter. But though this is too idealistic, there certainly needs to be a broad agreement on the basic principles, strategy and methods of church outreach to the world, under which full advantage may be taken of new ideas and developments. This would undoubtedly make for closer unity and oneness of purpose instead of the denominational rivalry and interdenominational competition which have marred so much missionary endeavour in the past.

The recent spate of congresses on evangelism, following the first held in Berlin, is full of encouragement. Singapore was the venue in 1970 for the All Asia Congress on Evangelism, in which Asian leadership became apparent. The All India Congress on Evangelism excluded all Western missionaries from its consultations, to demonstrate its ability and intention to assume the leadership in India's evangelization. The Philippines Congress on Evangelism asserted Filipino responsibility and the Thailand Congress on Evangelism for the first time awoke the

Thai church to its own potentialities. An earlier African Congress had similarly united evangelical churches with a common purpose to proclaim Christ.

But while we rejoice in these developments the task remains one for the whole church and closer links need to be forged between churches 'here' and 'there' and a system adopted which provides a constant two-way flow of information and a regular interchange of personnel between churches at home and overseas. In Great Britain the Evangelical Missionary Alliance is the body which is spear-heading the movement for informed and united action among interdenominational mission agencies. Its counterparts in North America are the Evangelical Foreign Missions Association and the Interdenominational Foreign Mission Association.

Church in conflict

The previous chapter has already outlined the unpredictable future of modern society in the light of exclusive nationalism, social tensions, revolutionary uprisings and the threat of wars. The church in some parts of the world has already been forced on to the defensive or even, as in China, been compelled to go completely underground. The day may be nearer than we think when missionary societies as they are now organized will no longer be able to function. We may not for long be able to dictate our own situations or the timing of our operations. Conventional methods in some areas could become impossible.

Perhaps, therefore, the church world-wide should be preparing strong-points, training infiltrators, organizing commandos, and setting up resistance movements in preparation for the 'evil day' (Ephesians 6:13). The church should always be ready to advance against the enemy when it has the advantage and to resist the enemy when the antagonism is stern. In situations which may arise in the future it is possible, though by no means certain, that Christians in secular employment may have an important role to play. But if so they too need to be trained in biblical strategy and to meet situations which they cannot fully anticipate. One thing seems certain, that when China opens its doors and the church within is liberated it will not be as missionaries or as members of a missionary society that Christians from abroad will return to China, if at all, but as those who are qualified to serve in some secular capacity as doctors, teachers, engineers, *etc.*, while identifying themselves with a local church.

Weapon of all prayer

The jargon of today speaks of 'strategic weapons'. The Christian's weapons, says Paul, are spiritual. Surely the weapon of 'all-prayer', rightly used, is the most strategic weapon of all. Moses' use of the weapon of 'all-prayer' against the Amalekites was as strategically important as Joshua's military strategy in the battle. The one without the other would have spelt defeat.

Today, besides mobilizing manpower to serve overseas, the church needs to mobilize its prayer support forces. The vital, indeed critical, importance of prayer must be emphasized continually. Societies should be more imaginative and inventive in stimulating individual intercession and in providing information and guidance for such intercessors. Group praying in many cases needs a breath of new life and rescuing from an old, unattractive image. Group leaders should display originality and imagination in keeping missionary prayer cells in colleges or elsewhere interesting and alive. A personal link between the group and an individual or with a society, a constant supply of topics for prayer (*e.g. Missionary Mandate*[1]), the occasional use of prayer tapes direct from workers overseas and film strips or slides are all invaluable aids to intelligent and informed prayer.

But prayer cannot be divorced from action. When it is, it tends to become a form of escape from reality. On the other hand, prayer harnessed to the right action is a weapon mighty through God to the pulling down of Satan's strongholds (2 Corinthians 10 : 4).

BIBLIOGRAPHY
Missionary Ideals by T. Walker, edited by David C. C. Watson (Inter-Varsity Press, 1969).
Missionary Methods, St. Paul's or Ours? by Roland Allen (Lutterworth Press, 1969).
Colonialism and Christian Missions by Stephen C. Neill (Lutterworth Press, 1966).

---

[1] Published six times a year. Apply Lancing Tabernacle, 1 Grand Avenue, Lancing, Sussex.

Revolution in Evangelism by W. Dayton Roberts (Scripture Union, 1968).
One Body, One Gospel, One World: the Christian Mission Today by Lesslie Newbigin (Edinburgh House Press, 1958).
Take Off Your Shoes by Michael Griffiths (Overseas Missionary Fellowship, 1971).
Theological Education by Extension edited by Ralph D. Winter (William Carey Library, South Pasadena, California, 1969).
An Introduction to the Science of Missions by J. Bavinck (Presbyterian and Reformed Publishing Co., 1960).
The Responsible Church and the Foreign Mission by P. Beyerhaus (World Dominion Press, 1964).
One World, One Task by the Evangelical Alliance Commission on World Mission (Scripture Union, 1971).

Problems to ponder
Planting a church in a multi-racial community

Background situation

Malaysia is a nation, the population of which is almost equally divided between Malays and Chinese. The Malays, however, are the ruling race. Tamils and animistic tribes are minority groups.

Malays are Muslims and protected by law from outside proselytization. The Chinese are Buddhists with superstitious animistic beliefs combined. The Tamils are Hindus.

Gemas is a busy railway junction town in South Malaya. The population consists of Muslim Malays, Hindu Tamils, Buddhist Hokkien and Hakka-speaking Chinese.

The bloody race riots of 1969, resulting from the Malay fear of Chinese power, left an atmosphere of fear and suspicion between the different races, causing them to isolate themselves from each other. They also emphasized to the Chinese that they are 'foreigners' and that China rather than Malaysia is their fatherland.

Because of unemployment and government policies which

discriminate against the Chinese and the Tamils in favour of the Malays in the allocation of jobs, Chinese and Indian young people are more and more moving to the larger towns to seek employment.

In 1967 there were two small groups of Christians in Gemas – one Chinese, consisting of six baptized believers and about six enquirers, and one Indian, consisting of two baptized be-believers and four or five members of a single family showing interest.

The objective

1. To teach the Christians the Word of God and to enable them to pass it on to others.

2. To create a church or fellowship sense among all Christians of each language group in Gemas.

The difficulties

1. *Religion.* Proselytization among Muslim Malays is forbidden by law. The keeping of Friday (Muslim Sunday) as the weekly 'rest day' in the State of Johore and of Sunday in the neighbouring State of Negri Sembilan (Gemas overlaps both states) makes difficulties in planning activities for all the people of the area. Chinese people usually work seven days per week for most of the daylight hours, allowing hardly any time for other activities.

2. *Tamil tradition.* Because the Tamil Christians belong to the labouring class by birth, other local Indians consider themselves to be of a higher caste and this creates a barrier. Teenage girls are kept at home and this makes it difficult to teach them and for them to teach others.

3. *Chinese tradition.* Because the Chinese believers are all solitary believers in heathen families, they are subjected to family pressures to conform to Buddhist and Confucianist family tradition. After the race riots Chinese Christians had a problem of allegiance resulting in feelings of isolation from other Chinese as well as from the Malays. There were pressures to conform for the sake of security.

4. *Education.* Only four or five of the Christians had more than a primary education, while several of the women in both

groups were illiterate. Several in the Tamil group were educated in both Tamil and English.

5. *Language*. With five languages or dialects spoken in the town (English, Malay, Tamil, Hokkien and Hakka), what is the missionary to do and what is to be the common language of communication? Ideally, the missionary should be able to speak two dialects of Chinese and Tamil if he is to communicate with all the groups. Alternatively, two or more missionaries are needed, each speaking different dialects or languages. Furthermore, recently (*i.e.* since 1969) the Government has been putting emphasis on the use of the National Language (viz. Malay) and each year the number of school subjects being taught through this medium is being increased. English is to be taught as a second language. This results, at present, in Chinese and Indian young people not being fluent in reading any language, and also lacking comprehension in any but Malay and their own dialect. Christian literature in Malay is still very limited, although several groups are now working on the preparation in this language of materials for Sunday School work.

6. *Employment*. Lack of educational facilities beyond Form 5 and lack of employment takes increasing numbers of young people away from country places into larger towns, leaving country churches bereft of leadership in youth work.

Quite a problem! *How would you tackle it?*

Possible approaches

1. Encourage Tamils and Chinese to meet and work together, using either English or Malay as a lingua franca.

2. Work separately within each of the three groups – two Chinese and one Tamil.

3. Teach each group separately in their own language, but encourage them to worship together and witness together.

The outworking

Method 3. was adopted because of:

1. the language problem.
2. the wide divergence in spiritual growth.

3. the need to realize and demonstrate their oneness in Christ.

Results

So far as the original group of Chinese Christians was concerned there was much disappointment. Most of them discontinued attending the mid-week prayer meeting and Bible study, so that compromise on the marriage question and unwillingness to set aside one day in the week for the Lord or to help in children's work or other outreach are not surprising.

However, there were six or more Chinese young people added to the number of believers during the period of missionary residence and quite a large number were known to be studying the Bible by correspondence course.

The eldest son (aged 19) in the Tamil family came to the Lord and was baptized in the first year of the period and has become one of the leaders of the work. The attitude of the Tamil Christians is in contrast to that of the Chinese. They are eager for fellowship and teaching. They meet each Saturday for two hours Bible study and prayer, become capable Sunday School teachers and are now responsible for running the Sunday School and training others. They attend and take part in a weekly worship service in English, all taking turns to lead and two of them regularly giving the message. They initiated a weekly Tamil service also in their own home, taking responsibility for leading and speaking. They are continually reaching out to others through personal witness, sale of Gospels, Christian magazines and distribution of tracts, and have been instrumental in leading other young people to the Saviour, several of whom are now preparing for baptism.

5
A world-changing gospel –
a revolutionary message

Gospel in a nutshell

Mark's guest-room in Jerusalem was full of frightened people when the Risen Christ suddenly appeared among them and in a few memorable sentences put the gospel in a nutshell: '... that the Christ should suffer and on the third day rise from the dead, and that repentance and forgiveness of sins should be preached in his name to all nations, beginning from Jerusalem....' In these pregnant phrases He helped them, in Luke's words, to 'understand the scriptures' (Luke 24: 46,47).

Paul, similarly, as a prelude to his great defence of the resurrection, pin-pointed the essentials of the apostolic gospel in these words: 'I delivered unto you as of first importance what I also received, that Christ died for our sins in accordance with the scriptures, that he was buried, that he was raised on the third day in accordance with the scriptures...' (1 Corinthians 15:3).

Unchanging human nature

The world and its technology have travelled far in 2,000 years. Man created in God's image has lofty capabilities, but he can also sink to great depths. To read Paul's description of human nature and human society in AD 60 and to compare that account with human society today, it is plain that human nature has not changed one little bit, certainly not for the better! (See Romans 1:26–32.) Paul writes of sexual perversion, marital unfaithfulness, fornication, covetous greed, crimes of violence, atheism, revolts against authority, *etc*. And he attributes man's moral and social degeneration entirely to his turning his back on God (Romans 1:21). Man in his natural state and whatever his religious tradition is lost – lost to God. His lost condition is seen not only in his irreligion or his man-made religion and in his immoral or amoral conduct, but also, as Hans Rookmaaker and Francis Schaeffer have pointed out, in his contemporary culture – in certain art forms and in some of the popular music of our time, all of which further emphasize the inexorable process of a disintegrating society. Man's alienation from God is the root cause of all personal, domestic and social dislocation. All social injustice and all human misery ultimately stem from man's rebellion against God and His laws – in other words, his sinfulness. Man's only hope for a better world is to discover a way to be reconciled, first to God and then to his fellow men, and thereafter to accept God's plan for the proper ordering of human life and society.

God's remedy
Christians are the only people who can present to the world with absolute authority an infallible answer to man's desperate need. Paul took a long, hard look at man in his desperation in his day, and then declared, 'I am not ashamed of the gospel: it (and it alone) is the power (the dynamite) of God for salvation to every one who has faith....' (Romans 1:16). He was proud to proclaim a revolutionary message for all mankind, the only message which could dynamite an old corrupt society and change the world by changing man first of all.

Unchanging gospel
Human nature has not changed. Man's need of God has not changed. Salvation is found in Christ alone on the ground of His death and resurrection. The command to proclaim Christ as the only way to God is still binding on the church as powerfully as ever. If God loves the world and offers eternal life to 'whoever' believes, then all must know of God's gift in order to be able to make their personal response (John 3:16). While it is literally true that Christ died for all, the Bible knows of no salvation without a personal response of faith in Him. Men are

83

not saved unconsciously without faith by reason of Christ's incarnation and atoning death alone. Indeed, men are described as lost until they believe in Christ. Salvation begins when man is reconciled to God and then continues throughout this life and on beyond death into eternity. The real 'apostolic succession' is that of those who faithfully preach the apostolic gospel in each succeeding generation. This apostolic gospel has never changed and can never change. Nevertheless a changing world and a changing climate of thought demand that the unchanging purposes of God be re-formulated in relation to the issues of today's world.

Other gospels
Paul used extremely strong language of those who would alter, detract from or add to the gospel which he preached as a divine revelation (Galatians 1:8,9). Already in his day there were men preaching a gospel of salvation dependent on the ritual of Jewish circumcision. Human nature has always preferred a system of salvation through a ritual or by self-effort – salvation through one's own good deeds – to a gospel which leaves him no possibility of saving himself (Ephesians 2:8,9). Indeed, self-effort is at the heart of all natural man-made religion. But Paul rejected both salvation by a church ritual and salvation by self-effort. He preached only a salvation through faith alone, without works and without ritual.

Secular Christianity
In the early part of this century, especially in the twenties after the First World War, there was much talk about the 'social gospel'. Christians were properly concerned about social conditions and quite rightly believed it to be a Christian's duty to fight injustice and the social causes of poverty and inequality. But gradually social action began to take the place of evangelism. Churchmen came to believe that it was more important to solve man's physical and social problems than to minister to his spiritual needs.

Today the gospel message, so clearly enunciated by our Lord and by the apostles, is being set aside. Even God Himself is considered to be an abstraction; the Personal God of the Christian tradition is dead! The resurrection of Christ is regarded by some theologians as a myth, rather than as an incontrovertible, historical event. Jesus is thus reduced to the status of a by-no-means infallible prophet. And so the gospel of the New Testament loses its credibility both as to its validity and as to its relevance in the world of today. In other words, the gospel is secularized. God is said to be operating in the secular world and can more readily be found there than in the church, according to Dietrich Bonhoeffer. The new emphasis on a 'revolutionary theology' goes beyond 'social work' for the alleviation of human suffering. It insists on 'social action' and involving the church in the movements which are changing social structures. Social action is an essential function of the church, but it cannot take the place of soul-winning and church expansion. 'The substitution of social action for evangelism poses one of the most serious long term threats to mission today' wrote Peter Wagner formerly of the Andes Evangelical Mission. But Christian social action must certainly follow or accompany evangelism or we come under the judgment of Scripture. According to Jesus, the naked must be clothed, and the hungry fed. 'Faith by itself, if it has no work, is dead' (James 2:14–17).

Uppsala 1969

The World Council of Churches meeting in Uppsala, Sweden, in 1969 was urged to adopt the 'agenda of the world' and to lead the churches forward in what was virtually a neo-Marxist programme of social change. The few evangelical voices raised in defence of the world-wide proclamation of the historic gospel of the grace of God were given a lukewarm, if not antagonistic, hearing.

'The Gospel for the whole man' is not a biblical expression, though the term expresses a truth implicit in Scripture. Man's nature cannot be dissected into parts; soul, spirit and body are one single person. We must not separate man into a spiritual part which is important and a material part which is not. Man is not just a 'soul with ears'. 'Saving souls' is equally an unbiblical expression, for Christ came to save the whole man and a salvation which does not affect the whole personality and the whole of life is an inadequate salvation. The gospel is more than individual, it is also more than social. God's salvation, therefore, has tremendous implications and applications to the social structures in which man lives and the church must certainly accept her full obligations for the world around. But that does not mean that she must substitute the 'agenda of the world' for the programme of Christ. Christianity is far more than humanitarianism.

Frankfurt Declaration

Alarmed at the trend of thinking at Uppsala among many of the world's leading churchmen, Professor Peter Beyerhaus and thirteen other theologians and scholars, all members of the 'Theological Convention' and also members of the World Council of Churches, in 1970 issued a document called 'The Frankfurt Declaration on the Fundamental Crisis in Christian Mission'. This document vigorously enunciated seven essentials of the historic gospel and point by point showed how that gospel conflicted with the current emphasis of the W.C.C. as expressed at Uppsala.

Some of the points made in this Frankfurt Declaration were these: 1. That since mission is grounded in the nature of the gospel, it is a mistake to determine the nature and task of mission by socio-political analyses of our time and from the demands of the non-Christian world. The surrender of the Bible as our primary frame of reference leads to the shapelessness of mission. 2. That it is contrary to the biblical revelation to suppose that Christ Himself is anonymously so evident in world religions, historical changes and revolutions that man can encounter Him and find salvation in Him without the direct news of the gospel. 3. That the universalistic idea that, in the death and resurrection of Jesus Christ, all men of all times are already born again and already have peace with Him, irrespective of their knowledge of the historical saving activity of God or belief in Him, is in direct conflict with the New Testament doctrine of the church's mission to the world. These points warrant a little further elaboration.

Syncretism

Syncretism denies that there is any unique revelation in history but maintains that there are many ways to reach divine reality. Syncretists also believe that all religious systems, all formulations of religious truth and all religious experience are inadequate expressions of truth and that it is therefore necessary to harmonize all such religious conceptions in order to arrive at a full understanding of the truth of religion. Syncretism has taken many forms through the centuries. It was a threat to Israel in the Old Testament. We detect it in the early church, sections of which apparently attempted to incorporate the ideas of the Gnostics into Christianity and so met with the powerful rebuttal of both the apostle Paul in Colossians (Jesus is pre-eminent) and of the apostle John in his Epistle. It crops up again in the humanism of the Renaissance. And now we meet with it once more in the search for a universal religion and the ecumenists' approach to other religions in search of a common agreement, in spite of Hendrik Kraemer's strong denunciation of syncretistic thinking in his address, 'The Christian message in the non-Christian World', to the World Council of Churches in 1938.

The gospel is unique. Christianity's central core of truth is that Jesus Christ is the only Saviour of men. Salvation cannot be found in any other religion, though elements of truth are there side by side with error. Nor has mystical experience anything directly to do with truth or with salvation. Sadhu Sundar Singh, the Indian Christian saint, had been a Hindu mystic before his conversion, but he frequently affirmed that his personal experience of life in Christ bore no resemblance to and had nothing in common with Hindu mysticism. Christ and the Christian gospel are unique, and in Christ are hid all the treasures of wisdom and knowledge, of philosophy and science. A syncretistic search for the completeness of truth by combining elements of truth in all religions is a false trail. 'I am the way, and the truth, and the life; no one comes to the Father, but by me,' said Jesus (John 14:6).

Anonymous Christianity

Some contemporary missionary theologians, Protestant and Roman Catholic, have become fascinated with the idea that, through the merits of Christ's incarnation and crucifixion, all men throughout the world are in fact already saved, though they may not know it. Christ is already present in men's hearts and beliefs, even before they hear the gospel. This is the concept known as 'anonymous Christianity'. There is no suggestion here of syncretism. Salvation, it is agreed, is through Christ and His sacrifice alone. But to avoid accepting the harsh alternative that the godless who have died down the centuries have perished and that those living today without a knowledge of Christ will do so, it is suggested that Christ's saving work covers them all, just as it presumably covers an innocent child or an imbecile.

In reply to the criticism that such a belief cuts the nerve of evangelism, the holders of this theory affirm that the major motive for evangelization is not and has never been 'the lost state of the heathen' but simple obedience to God's imperative command to preach the gospel to all nations. And in any case those enjoying the present blessings of salvation should surely want the rest of the world to enjoy them too in experience. But this theory ignores or by-passes those New Testament passages which insist on a personal faith in Christ as the only way of salvation, and the awful destiny of those who die unbelieving. 'Anonymous Christianity' virtually becomes a new version of the unscriptural doctrine of universalism – the teaching that all men will eventually be saved.

The new missiologists believe that 'the motive of missions is not to be located in a belief that the lack of explicit faith in Jesus automatically determines a man's final destiny. We cannot make any such assertions' (Victor Hayward). Since the whole of mankind is redeemed and Christ is Lord of all it is no longer appropriate, we are told, to say 'repent or perish'; the message is 'Christ is your Lord, whether you know it or not!' Thus the idea of a one-by-one process of personal faith is now regarded as out-moded.

The great commission

Christ's commission to His church to evangelize the nations is repeated in varying form and emphasis by all four Evangelists and again by Luke in the Acts. It is rightly regarded as the church's charter. The church is certainly a Christian fellowship, a worshipping fellowship. But neither fellowship nor worship are the primary *raisons d'être* of the church. They are both the pre-requisites and prelude to evangelism or witness. There is much truth in the current catch phrase, 'The Church is mission', though admittedly it is an over-simplification. But mission is not just mission in far-off places; it is mission at home – in our own 'Jerusalem' first of all, then to the uttermost parts of the earth. And if your home happens to be in Japan, then for you the uttermost part of the earth or 'the very ends of the earth' (J. B. Phillips) might be Great Britain!

While these responsibilities are binding on the whole Christian church and therefore on all its members everywhere, not just a select few, it was not apparently mere obedience to this particular decree that was the overriding motive of the early Christians. Rather, the Holy Spirit, the Spirit of Christ and the Spirit of evangelism, was the driving force, the consuming passion, the flaming fire which thrust them out from Jerusalem to Judea, from Judea to Samaria, and from Samaria to the ends of the earth (Acts 1:8). The church, to be true to herself and her Lord and in obedience to the urge of her own inner life, must keep on going at all costs and never stop until the end of the age and the return of Christ.

Nevertheless the great commission ringing clearly in their ears must certainly have profoundly influenced the actions of the apostles who heard it from the Saviour's own lips on the Mount of Olives, His last memorable words. The history of their programme as recorded in the Acts is surely to be seen as the way in which the apostles interpreted the terms of the great commission. There is far more to it than a simple command to 'go and evangelize'.

An analysis of its terms (Matthew 28:18–20) clearly reveals: 1. its objective – 'make disciples'; 2. its scope – 'all nations'; 3. its focus – 'baptizing', *i.e.* membership of the church; 4. its doctrinal foundation – 'the Triune God'; 5. its method – 'teaching ... all ...', *i.e.* a comprehensive syllabus of instruction; 6. its inspiration – 'I am with you', *i.e.* the abiding presence of Christ; 7. its duration – 'to the close of the age'; 8. its dynamic – 'all authority', *i.e.* the power promised by the ascended Christ. Without this (*cf.* Acts 1:8) everything else will fail. And that is why our Lord prefaced His commission with these words; we should also give them the same priority in our thinking, prayer and action.

This programme is as valid and practicable in the 1970s as in the first century. We must avoid the temptation of thinking that our changing times demand any basic change in objectives and methods. In one sense everything in the world has changed and is changing. In another sense nothing has changed. The greatest need in the world today is not, as many think, the sophisticated specialist but the dedicated Christian who will make disciples, baptize them, gather congregations, and teach Christians to be effective in their families, communities and national society as a whole.

Proclamation or dialogue

The emphasis of the New Testament is on proclamation, preaching and teaching and implies a profound conviction that Christ is the unique and only way to God (John 14:6). Conversation, discussion and dialogue can all supplement proclamation as a way to achieving a greater mutual understanding of the Christian and non-Christian positions. 'Gossiping the gospel' in the coffee-house has its value as well as preaching in the market-place. But there can be no question of compromise between revealed truth and human speculation, no sacrificing of Christian convictions and no surrendering of the right and duty to proclaim Jesus Christ as the only Saviour of men.

Christian presence

Nothing can be more important than a quality of life on the messenger's part, if the message is to be substantiated. Christians have often failed miserably just here through inconsistent living. There is great value in the physical presence of the Christian in a non-Christian community if others can thereby see Christ lived out in human lives and through good works

(Matthew 5:16). But this kind of 'Christian presence' can never be a substitute for the verbal proclamation of Christ and the explanation of the way of salvation. No Christian presence witnessing in life can be enough. Without the explanation, the Philippian jailor would have been left amazed at the lives and testimonies of Paul and Silas but ignorant of the nature of the power that lay behind it (Acts 16:30, 31). The silent witness may be all that is possible under some circumstances, but a silent presence can never lead people to faith in Christ. 'How are they to believe in him of whom they have never heard? And how are they to hear without a preacher?' (Romans 10:10).

The evangelization of the world is, as it has always been, the most glorious, the most essential, and the most God-glorifying task entrusted to man. The privilege of proclaiming Christ world-wide in whatever capacity remains the highest and noblest of all callings. The risen Christ still stands among His own people and His voice still speaks with divine compulsion saying to this generation, as to generations past, 'Go into all the world and preach the gospel to the whole creation' (Mark 16:15) – and in the power of the Holy Spirit (Acts 1:8). As Michael Griffiths wrote in *Voice* (Spring 1971), Christians overseas are 'guerilleros' – numerically insignificant and poorly equipped irregulars working for a revolution in men's hearts. 'We want to see a *coup d'état* in the heart of individual after individual, the reign of Christ established in men's hearts now, and the establishment of Christian cell groups, part of that new secret society which one day will be a glorious church. . . .'

BIBLIOGRAPHY
Frontiers in Modern Theology by Carl F. H. Henry (Moody Press, 1966).
Secular Christianity by Ronald Gregor Smith (Collins, 1966).
Pentecost and Missions by Harry R. Boer (Lutterworth Press, 1961).
Message and Mission by Eugene A. Nida (Hamish Hamilton, 1960).
'Secular Christianity' and the God who Acts by Robert J. Blaikie (Hodder and Stoughton, 1970).
Christianity and Comparative Religion by J. N. D. Anderson (Tyndale Press, 1970).
The Unchanging Commission by David Adeney (Inter-Varsity Press, 1961).
Christian Faith and Other Faiths by Stephen Neill (Oxford University Press, 1970).

Problems to ponder
How to start evangelizing a primitive tribe

Background situation

In the Amazon basin of Brazil there are numerous 'Indian' tribes living under primitive conditions. The Kaiwa tribe is found in the south-west of Brazil close to the Paraguayan border, some of the people actually living in Paraguay and crossing the border frequently.

The terrain consists of gallery forest interspersed with savannah and the Indians call themselves 'forest people'. The area has been heavily penetrated by Brazilian settlers.

There are about 7,000 members of the tribe, of whom 2,500 are more or less permanently settled on government reservations in Brazil and another 2,000 scattered on Brazilian farms. The remainder are in Paraguay. The Indians move around a lot within an area of about 750 square miles, including an international frontier. Some live in isolated pockets among the Brazilian estates.

Christianity and the Kaiwa

1. *Political status*. The Kaiwa are considered to be 'minors' of the state and so have no political rights. Their land is not individually owned but is the property of the Indian Foundation, which exercises a paternal protection over them. In extreme cases they are outrageously exploited and used as 'slave labour' by their 'protectors', the representatives of a 'Christian' government.

2. *Social status*. The worst enemy of the Kaiwa, as of all the Indian tribes, is their image; the Brazilians have a very low opinion of the Indian and his potentiality. Even Brazilian Christians doubt if the Indian has a soul! The Indian generally is considered to be at an intermediate stage between animal and human. Until recently, government policy has been entirely non-progressive and bedevilled by a low view of the Indian. Decimation by disease has been largely checked by the magnificent work of the Kaiwa Mission, now entirely in Brazilian

hands, and by government help. However, the Indian generally speaking continues to be a marginal, largely discouraged or apathetic person. Many, however, are still fiercely proud and searching for identity. The only role that they can see for themselves in Brazilian life simply does not attract them. Some Indians live almost deliberately in a very primitive fashion. The Indian lives on good land and the area is littered with the wreckage of projects that have been started to help 'the poor Indian'. Since these have always been from outside, with promises rarely kept, they have all been rejected and the Indian is bitter and disillusioned. Nor can he trust his neighbour. Being on good land, the Indians should recover their old community work habits and work for themselves, but they cannot trust each other any more. The lazy sponge off the active to the point where it is not worth anyone's time to work hard. The result is that the men troop off to the Brazilian farms to earn a pittance. Even when they are not abused their earnings do not really help them, because they spend them on drink or trinkets.

3. *Religion*. Rather than become simply very poor Brazilians, the Indians prefer to be despised Indians and cling tenaciously to their religion as something which is distinctive and gives them links with the past. Their religion is that of animism or the worship of spirits in a variety of ways.

4. *Christianity and the Kaiwa*. The Kaiwa were visited by the Jesuits in the sixteenth and seventeenth centuries, but proved very resistant to the Faith, even though, or perhaps because, the Roman Catholics executed recalcitrant witch doctors. The Kaiwa took over some of the externals – the cross, altar and vestments – but these were bereft of any Christian content. There is a 'mother of god' in their mythology. Baptism is practised, but merely means to 'receive a Brazilian name'. Some use saints as charms. But this is the extent of Roman Catholic influence.

How would you tackle this situation? (Discuss.)

Present objective in reaching the Kaiwa

1. To take the gospel to the Kaiwa and to plant churches.

2. To provide the Kaiwa with as much Scripture translated into their own language as is necessary for church growth and

evangelism within the tribe and without dependence on outside spiritual help (*i.e.* the New Testament, and Old Testament background).

3. To provide reading and educational materials and to train Kaiwa teachers (*i.e.* to produce a 'climate' within which the Bible will be maximally used by ongoing generations).

4. To encourage community development as the tribe begins to be changed by the Book and guided by the Spirit and to show them that they do not need to become 'poor Brazilians' in order to become Christians.

Alternative methods

1. To evangelize the Kaiwa by using the Portuguese language or the Guarani lingua franca.

Modern attempts to do so have tended to downgrade Indian language, culture and music. All the Kaiwa holds dear and important has been scoffed at, which has only served to make the Indian insecure in Brazilian society and, if he becomes a 'Christian', to do so merely outwardly, while remaining a pagan at heart. Since the Indians are such a disintegrated people, the short-cut of using Portuguese would accomplish nothing in depth and would simply make it harder to help the Indian realize that he has worth and is quite capable of being a leader and teacher of his own people (even though the Brazilians do not think so!).

2. To evangelize the Kaiwa in their own language.

Case history

1. Mr and Mrs X and their children moved into a Kaiwa settlement and lived simply in a tribal-style house in close contact with the villagers – lives open for all to see.

2. They set about learning the language aided by modern linguistic techniques.

3. They began to translate portions of Scripture with the aid of local informants. So far (1971) two books of Scripture have been completed, a set of reading primers is already in a second edition and a reader containing more advanced reading material is in print.

Results to date

A slow but increasing interest, but so far no church. Mr X says: 'Personally I have never been in a situation where it is so obvious that nothing can happen until there is a real spiritual renewal and the Indians are prepared to take the initiative guided by the Spirit. When they start to move we will be able to help them. So our continuing aim is to get the gospel to them in their language and to show them that they do not need to turn into the poorest of Brazilians in order to be Christians.'

6
Meeting the world's need —
the means available

Then and now

It is difficult for us in the twentieth century to imagine how we would have gone about evangelizing the world in the first century — without cars, without aeroplanes, without printing presses, without loud-speakers or microphones, without radio and television, without cameras, without typewriters, without duplicators, without adding machines or computers, without a postal system, without anaesthetics and brain surgeons. No quick travel, no books or magazines, no Christian broadcasting, no aseptic hospitals, no prophylactic protection against killer diseases, no means of visualizing what other parts of the world were like, no well-equipped offices! None of these was essential to the proclamation of the gospel then, nor are they now! They are modern tools, but nothing more.

The apostle Paul probably walked or rode a donkey on his missionary travels, when he did not travel by sea. His letters were written by an amanuensis and carried by personal messenger. His reading matter was confined to the Septuagint Old Testament and some favourite parchments. When he preached to large audiences he simply 'lifted up his voice'. He carried no cheap, subsidized Bibles to give to converts. The Gospel of John did not even exist. And yet the gospel was proclaimed in ever-widening circles. More and more churches were planted. The flame spread. The Ethiopian eunuch took the gospel to Africa, the apostle Thomas took it to India, and Augustine took it to Britain.

Today, provided with travel facilities of every kind and

armed with a complex variety of gadgets and techniques, the church has no excuse for failure. We shall consider seven invaluable aids to the proclamation of the gospel. To list them in order of priority is impossible, so we take them in alphabetical order.

Bible translation

Paul could and did read his Hebrew Bible in the Greek Septuagint translation. During his widespread missionary travels his language for communicating the gospel, whatever the local language or dialect might have been, was Greek. Greek was the only existing translation of the Bible (Old Testament) in the apostolic times.

'The latest count of languages in which at least some part of the Scriptures is available is 1,413 – covering no less than 97% of the world's population. That still leaves upwards of 1,500 languages to go. Those remaining languages belong mostly to very small population groups; for example, 650 out of 700 languages spoken in Papua, New Guinea. But remember that 3% of the world's population still means well over 90,000,000 people. So we have new languages to work in, the number growing all the time' (British and Foreign Bible Society Report, June 1970). Many of the older translations by present standards are poor and, as in Laos, entirely new translations are in progress.

Modern language-learning techniques, scientific language analysis and the use of computers are speeding up the process of Bible translation. Experts hold translation institutes all over the world, such as the one held in February 1971 in Bangkok for ninety translators and a dozen 'informants' from South-East Asia and Pakistan. Then 'the marriage of Biblical scholarship with the new science of linguistics ... has given us the means of conveying the original meaning of the Bible writers more precisely and intelligibly than ever before' (*ibid.*).

It is a thrilling thing to translate the Scriptures for the first time. Line upon line, verse after verse, chapter after chapter, book after book until the whole Bible is complete. In 1970 two such completed Bibles went into print for the first time – the Lisu Bible for Burma and China, and the Ogori Bible for

Nigeria. The Lisu Bible took over fifty years, from start to finish, to complete. But in many languages the work is still in its early stages. Though future generations may be educated in a single national language which, as 'Indonesian' is doing in Indonesia, will eventually displace the local vernacular languages, the need to provide the present generation with some portions of Scripture in their own tongue is essential to the building of healthy local churches. Bible translation is not an end in itself, but it is an essential means to this end.

Cassettophones and Gospel Recordings

For many years Gospel Recordings have been producing simple evangelistic statements in hundreds of languages on records which, with a simple hand-wound gramophone, have taken the truth and repeated it over and over again in the voices of their own people to hundreds and thousands of people in every continent. The arrival of the inexpensive cassettophone now makes it possible to provide several hours of teaching on a single tape instead of the few minutes possible on a record. The possibilities of this new development for building Christ's church are enormous.

Christian education

Illiteracy and ignorance have plagued the world for long enough. Those who translate the Scriptures must also conduct literacy campaigns to teach the people to read what they have translated. But even literacy campaigns are only the beginning, if the church is to become an educated church. In point of fact general education overseas has always arrived with the gospel. But in the church a secular education cannot be isolated from the whole strategy of Christian education, namely the total educational task of the church 'to present every man perfect in Christ Jesus' and to ensure a literate and enlightened Christian community.

But what place does education have as an evangelistic agency? The provision of education to Christians where no other educational opportunities exist is clearly an essential task, but opinion differs about using Christian schools as direct evangelistic agencies. David Gitari of Kenya says emphatically: 'It is wrong for a teacher to think of school as an evangelistic medium. He is first and foremost a teacher, though the whole of his personality is Christ-orientated.' Too much pressure on children in school to become Christian has doubtful long-term results and may just as easily lead to rebellion. At the same time, the committed Christian teacher cannot but live the Christian life and bring in his own point of view in all sorts of ways, both inside and outside the classroom. He will gain more respect if he has prepared his charges for life in general as well as made the gospel clear to them. In most parts of Africa and also elsewhere in the world there are still numerous openings for Christian teachers in secular schools where they can profoundly influence the rising generation. Their own personal witness will be important, but obviously active proselytization in government schools will usually not be tolerated.

Christian education is costly. Some missions have in the past allowed their educational programme to fill too large a place in relation to direct evangelism. In a broad sense mission schools have made a great contribution to the backward nations of the world in helping them to achieve increasing literacy and in educating their young men and women for community and national leadership. But judged by the standard of gaining converts and building churches, results have on the whole not been commensurate with the large sums of money spent and the big proportion of personnel involved. Even in Christian education, the goal of church building and church growth must be kept clearly in focus (see appendix to Chapter 2).

Films

Over thirty years ago the film 'King of Kings' was shown in many parts of China and made a deep impression. Today in Laos and elsewhere in South-East Asia a present generation of pagans are being impressed by the same film. But now Christian agencies are producing films and using this medium on a large scale. All the Fact and Faith Films produced by the Moody Institute of Science have had an almost world-wide circulation. In Japan they have been seen by millions on television. Unfortunately too many of the present films are of Western origin and were made for Western audiences. Even a dubbed-in synchronized sound track in a local language cannot really compensate for this. The scope for national Christian film companies making their own evangelistic films in countries where thousand still flock to see films in the open air is large.

Literature

In most continents, Christian literature production has been a late starter, the Cinderella of missions. Much was done in China before 1945, but little by the evangelical societies which only woke up to the urgency of the need when it was too late. In Latin America, however, literature was a pioneer medium from the beginning. Evangelical work there was actually commenced by Bible Society colporteurs. Now literature is being given high priority by mission agencies and by national churches in every continent. Indication of the growing concern was the All Asian Literature Strategy Conference held in 1970 in Singapore which drew together Asians from fifteen Asian countries engaged in literature work to consult about future plans. Asians were determined to take the fullest responsibility and no longer to leave it to the missionaries.

In West Africa too, the Africa Christian Press of Ghana is leading the way by publishing books by Africans for Africans. In Zaire, LECO is a publishing house supported by some twenty-three missions which has tripled its production of Christian books to meet the need in over 150 Zaire languages. The Christian Literature Association in Malawi (CLAIM) is a fellowship of about fourteen groups involved in Christian literature work. Nor are these all, by any means. In 1971 an Africa-wide Christian Committee Congress was held in Kenya when half the leaders were Africans and fifteen African leaders shared the platform. In Latin America, the churches lay great stress on literature; there are 148 evangelical book stores in Brazil, all members of the Brazil Chamber of Evangelical Literature. In Argentina, a mobile book van tries to compensate for the lack of Christian bookshops. Chile, too, where a Marxist government is now in power, has bookshops in Santiago and in Concepción, both bases for colportage trips into the remote north and throughout the length of the country. The West Indies have many evangelical bookshops and, like *Africa Challenge, Carib-*

bean Challenge is a monthly magazine which reaches fifty different countries and is meeting a great need. But everywhere personnel, especially nationals, are in short supply.

It was Gandhi's nephew who jibed, 'You missionaries taught us to read, but the Communists provided the reading material.' Many missions and literature agencies are now trying desperately to remove that stigma and to make up for lost time. 'An ounce of ink makes people think!' it has been said. But what thoughts? Pure or impure? False or true? Mao's or God's? Pornographic as well as Communist literature is widely available on the secular bookstalls of the world, but little that is Christian. The potential, therefore, in literature production and distribution is enormous, but it will require large capital investment, trained national writers, expert translators, artists, printers and businessmen, all on a large scale. There can be no limit to the scope of this enterprise so long as there are 1,000,000 new readers in the world every day with a great thirst for reading material. Take all the London publishing firms together and even they would be inadequate to meet the vast and expanding need for high quality literature in the Third World.

The West enjoys its huge libraries of doctrinal, theological and devotional literature. Elsewhere the total available books of this nature are pitifully few. Pastors often have virtually no library of doctrinal and devotional books at all. Overseas Christians have access to few Christian books compared with those who live in the favoured West. Books and more books of every variety are urgently needed, wherever a Christian church has been planted and where there are Christians able to read.

But where are the books to come from? Translations of literature from the West have their value if the translations are well done. A great many are not. There is a vast need for Westerners who can communicate ideas — good writers, effective journalists, professional script-writers. But nothing can take the place of writing by national authors. Unfortunately these do not grow overnight; they must first have something to say, and that implies spiritual maturity. Then they must know how to say it, and that means skilled training in journalism, laborious research and adequate financial backing. Unfortunately in most countries, such as in Indonesia, the financial rewards for Christian writers are small and many potential Christian writers turn to secular work. Training and encouraging writers is a major task for Western journalists and writers. Schools of journalism are needed in every country.

Literature production may be one bottle-neck, but distribution is a far greater one. Most churches are not yet literature-minded. They must be helped to become so. Bookshops multiplied a thousand-fold must then provide the facilities and books to meet what will be a growing need. Every missionary should be a 'literature missionary' in the sense of encouraging Christians to read and introducing them to the appropriate books.

Evangelistic literature (*i.e.* tracts or leaflets) is a different aspect of the problem. As a weapon in the hands of a skilled Christian worker literature is good; but without personal, face-to-face communication, it is very limited in its usefulness. It is doubtful whether mere literature distribution without person-to-person contact deserves to be called evangelism at all. 'Tracting' is so often a substitute for real contact and friendship. It is at best a superficial means of evangelism, though some are undoubtedly converted as a result. But for a jeep to roar through a village scattering gospel tracts to the inhabitants and then for the jeep's occupants to claim that they have 'evangelized' the village is a ludicrous caricature of evangelism. It has been done! By placing a tract in every home, claims have been made to have evangelized the whole nation! The real question is – were they read? and if so, were they understood? The Ethiopian eunuch could not understand Isaiah 53 until Philip explained it to him.

Much therefore depends on the quality of the presentation in the tract or leaflet. Preferably, again, these should not be translations of Western tracts, but the work of nationals, so ensuring that the truth is conveyed in familiar thought-patterns and with the right cultural expression.

When we stop to think of all that we owe to Christian literature it should be clear that the best way to repay that debt is to ensure that millions of new readers around the world should be able to share the privileges which we in the West so richly enjoy.

Medicine

Christian missions were the pioneers of medicine in many parts of the world. It was missionary doctors and nurses who first brought healing to the people of China and trained the first Chinese doctors and nurses. In India it was the same story; great missionary eye surgeons and leprologists, as well as countless devoted medical missionaries, have been committed to meeting the physical and spiritual needs of disease-ridden undernourished masses. In India and in China, missions have set up world-renowned medical schools – the Peking Union Medical College in China, Vellore and Ludhiana in India. Africa too, from the days of Dr David Livingstone, has had its honourable history of medical missions, often working in close co-operation with colonial governments. Then, all over the world, Christian missionaries have been the pioneers in the treatment and care of leprosy. They have also been foremost in the research which has resulted in potent new drugs which can actually cure the disease and have even brought within man's reach the possibility of eliminating the disease from the world entirely. The leprosy field is one in which Christian doctors and nurses will always have a predominant ministry. There are altogether approximately 180 Christian medical agencies responsible for 12,000 doctors to man the world's Christian institutions. Inevitably there is some duplication of effort.

Christian medical work overseas must, like everything else, adjust itself to changing times. It is questionable whether mission hospitals should try to compete with the new medical services now being provided by governments. It may prove strategic to move old-established hospitals to new areas as yet uncatered for by governments. But even so, the time is past, according to Dr Robert Cochrane, the veteran leprologist, for medical missionaries to wear themselves out trying to meet all the vast medical need. Ultimately this task is one for governments to undertake. The day of the one doctor bush hospital is also passing. Christian hospitals of the future, in co-ordination with government programmes, should be places for training and models of what an efficient, caring medical programme ought to be. They may be fewer in number, but they would also be better staffed and equipped and therefore larger. Their aim should be, not to meet all the need around, but to demonstrate how that need can be met. In this way they will reproduce themselves in others. As Dr Cochrane says, 'Medical missionary work is a temporary measure, undertaken by the Church until such time as the country concerned is able to organize a more comprehensive service for its people and able to give medical and health service to all.'

Attention is also moving from curative to preventive medicine. Public health schemes are ones in which Christian doctors and nurses should play a larger part. Clinics for this purpose, conducted by itinerating teams of medicals and evangelists, present great possibilities without the high costs of running modern hospitals. Programmes for rural, low-level training of dispensers and lay orderlies, in conjunction with a central hospital, and itinerating medical teams are indicated. A missionary doctor in Nigeria reasons, 'The most persuasive argument in favour of curative efforts is the humanitarian appeal of thousands of sick children who daily besiege clinics and hospitals in urgent need of treatment. The most potent argument in favour of preventive efforts is the certain knowledge that their wide application will, in the long run, reduce more effectively the over-all morbidity and mortality rates.'

The danger to watch is the growth of costly institutions where the use of personnel and finances are out of proportion to those used in church planting work; and situations where the hospitals overshadow or monopolize the local church should if possible be avoided. (See appendix to this chapter.)

Radio and television
In a world whose population is multiplying so alarmingly probably the only way by which every living person can be reached with the Christian message is through radio and television. In Japan and North America, time for Christian radio and television can easily be bought on commercial or government stations. Local radio is being extensively used by the churches in Indonesia and Latin America. In other countries, such as Great Britain, radio and TV are a government monopoly and no-one can buy time for Christian broadcasting. Broadcasts from Christian stations can therefore be heard in Great Britain only from

foreign stations. However there are those working with the BBC who are endeavouring to inject more positive Christian content into religious programmes, and the arrival of local radio stations in Great Britain may provide new and strategic opportunities for local Christians with adequate training and experience to provide first-class religious programmes.

In some countries, however, it is possible to set up private radio stations. Since 1945 when KCJB, the Voice of the Andes, the first-ever missionary radio station, began broadcasting in Colombia, about sixty missionary radio stations have come into operation and are covering the world with ever more powerful and effective signals. The Far East Broadcasting Company with its headquarters in Manila is third only to Radio Moscow and Radio Peking in the number of broadcasting hours it puts out per week in forty languages. That virtually the whole world is able to tune in to these programmes has been facilitated by the cheap transistor radio, now the common status symbol from the Khyber Pass to the Amazon jungle. In 'black' Africa in 1955 there were fewer than 400,000 radios; today there are upward of 6,000,000. In Japan, where there are 52,000,000 radios, 75% of the poulation can now hear the daily network programme of the Pacific Broadcasting Association which is sponsored by churches and missions in Japan. Throughout the world there are more than 500,000,000 radios. It is only through radio that the message can penetrate 'closed lands' such as China, and minister to the needs of Christians while reaching non-Christians as well. There is no spot on the globe today where the gospel of Jesus Christ is not heard by way of long-wave or short-wave radio ranging in power from a few thousand watts to super-powered transmitters of 100,000 watts. There are, however, not a few difficulties still to be surmounted – weak signals, the lack of short-wave receivers in many lands and of short-wave-bands on many sets, crowded wave-bands and, not least, poor programming by evangelical stations.

TV too is rapidly becoming universal. According to Television Digest Fact Book in New York, television is watched in 131 countries on over 270,000,000 sets. Even the hill tribes of Taiwan have become regular viewers. In Japan, 98,000,000 people regularly watch TV and a great many of these have seen the Moody Fact and Faith series of films with a Japanese sound-track. In 1970 Luis Palau, a Latin American evangelist, preached to 700,000 TV viewers on Mexico's most powerful station. Following this, 64 TV stations in Latin America commissioned a thirteen-week series of Christian films in Spanish.

But what of the future? 'With sophisticated missile circuitry and using the ubiquitous transistor, TV sets will be as common and cheap as radio sets. Video-tapes will soon be upon us. Some day we may wear a TV set like a wrist-watch and have it energized by bodily heat. Pioneers in Christian television will soon find themselves at the centre of the action in Christianity today. Needed are artists, musicians, engineers, announcers, technicians, actors, camera-men, photographers, producers, writers, reporters, film librarians and editors, specialists in lighting, costuming and make-up. The really great frontiers for Christianity today lie in the air' (*International Christian Broadcasters Bulletin*, February 1969).

But China is a good example of what is the greatest need in Christian broadcasting today – greatly improved programming. Some of the present programmes heard in China would appear to most listeners to be either incomprehensible or irrelevant. Programmes need to be aware of China's new culture and aware of the Marxian framework of the life and thought in China today. Christian broadcasts can be received in China from Korea, Taiwan, Okinawa, Hongkong and Manila, but only if these programmes are up to professional standards and relevant to the listeners will the message be not only transmitted but also received and understood. Only high quality and imaginative programmes win and hold audiences unfamiliar with the thought and vocabulary of Christianity. The competition with the popular secular programmes will not easily be won. It is too easy to switch off, or to turn to another station, if Christian programmes are not of sufficient interest to hold their listeners. And so, for every engineer needed, ten people are needed in the programming field.

But how can Christian radio and television grow churches? Ideally, interested listeners to Christian radio should be followed up, as with the Pacific Broadcasting Association in Japan, by personal contact, radio rallies and correspondence courses. Listeners who write in ought also to be put in touch with local churches. But, in the absence of such facilities in many areas of the world, most people who would never otherwise have the opportunity of hearing the gospel, especially in Communist countries where open evangelism is forbidden, can, if they wish or dare to, hear the gospel by radio. The possible future use of communication satellites will bring more and more of the world's population within hearing of the gospel. If there are those who consider broadcasting and literature too costly enterprises, then let them remember those who valued their herd of swine more than a single human soul! World outreach can no longer be promoted on a cut-rate budget. The easy, cheap ways of missionary work are gone for ever.

Means and the end
In considering all these means at our disposal it would be disastrous to confuse the means with the end. This is the grave error into which many missions have fallen in the past; to regard Bible translation as an end in itself, as the be-all and end-all of contemporary mission work; or to place a primary emphasis on education which by its very nature is costly and therefore in danger of dominating the thinking and planning of mission leaders. Radio and TV easily fire the imagination of the Christian public, and publicity for these invaluable means sometimes appears to infer that they have displaced the old methods of evangelism and church planting; they all too easily become an end in themselves and divert financial support to themselves and away from the basic, though less glamorous activities of a church-planting programme. Likewise literature, to the importance of which missionaries have awakened so late, has sometimes been given a publicity which suggests that *this* is the last word in world evangelization. Good quality Christian literature is, of course, an aid, an essential aid, in an evangelistic programme and invaluable for establishing and building up Christians in their faith. But it is no substitute for the hard-slogging, often slow programme of planting and nurturing local churches.

To mistake the means for the end and to confuse tactical weapons with grand strategy is to frustrate God's plan of mission. Let us beware of all exaggerated claims about the role of the specialist today and the declining usefulness of the church planter. We certainly do not desire to canonize the *status quo,* but with all our modern awareness of a changing world and of the changes needed in church/mission relationships, our greatest need is to return to the first principles of New Testament example and strategy. None of the mechanical or electronic media – printing press, radio, television – will ever adequately substitute for the incarnation of the gospel by the visible Christian community in the evangelization of the world. God's method, or medium, is now, as ever, 'the Word made flesh'.

And there is something else too. Great musicians have often been successful teachers, whose pupils have themselves become famous. The renowned pianist Moseivitch, who owed much to his own teachers and indirectly something to the teaching of Beethoven, was once interviewed on BBC TV by John Freeman in the 'Face to Face' series of programmes. John Freeman asked him if he had ever taught the piano to pupils. 'No,' he replied. 'I am a concert pianist, not a teacher !' A few weeks later he died. It seemed very sad that all his skills and techniques had died with him. He had taught no-one else and passed on none of his inherited and natural skills to others.

In the past, missionaries have too often been the good solo performers, the concert pianists, who have occupied the stage, had the spot-light focused on them and received all the applause. But they have failed to see the great importance of teaching others and of passing on their own skills, techniques and 'know-how' to national Christians. Don't let us repeat those mistakes today ! As well as translating the Scriptures ourselves, priority should be given to training Africans and Asians to become translators. Training school teachers is in the long run more strategic than teaching oneself, whether at Sunday School level or in a teacher training college. In the sphere of radio and television it is too easily assumed that only Europeans and Americans can do the job, whereas our greatest contribution will be in training nationals, both as engineers and as script-writers, programmers and broadcasters. In literature, too, the sooner Africans and Asians take over from missionaries the production and distribution of Christian literature the better.

Western missionaries should be deliberately and painstakingly working towards this end – training journalists, business managers, and colporteurs, while enthusing the churches of the world about the important place literature should have in their programmes.

At the All-Asian Literature Strategy Conference to which reference has already been made, 97 Asian representatives of Christian literature agencies in fifteen Asian countries took part. In an eight-point declaration the following is significant: 'We declare that we will take immediate steps to place nationals in positions of leadership in our literature agencies and that where national leadership is not available we will take adequate steps to develop it in the shortest possible time.'

This is the way ahead, not only for literature, but for every other activity on behalf of the churches of the world. It is high time that missionaries ceased to be the concert pianists; they should step down from the stage and leave it to others whom they have taught; writers, engineers, translators, nurses, script-writers and publishing-house directors. All these in turn must be clearly taught that the means is not the end and that the medium, whatever it is, must always be kept strictly subservient to the main objective.

BIBLIOGRAPHY
Two Thousand Tongues to Go by E. E. Wallis and M. A. Bennett (Hodder and Stoughton, 1966).
An Annotated Bibliography related to the Field of Christian Radio compiled by Susan Wardrop.
World Missions Handbook (Evangelical Missionary Alliance, 1969. New edition in preparation).
Missions in the Seventies by Dennis Clark (Scripture Union, 1970).

Problems to ponder
Christian hospitals, their use and limitations

Background

1. *Political*. Thailand, formerly Siam, is a nation of 33,000,000 people having frontiers with Burma, Laos, Cambodia and Malaysia. Unlike these and other South-East Asian nations Thailand, proudly meaning 'Freeland', has never known Western colonial rule. Consequently this intensely patriotic and graciously mannered people consider none their superior, and tend to pity the large, ungainly, comparatively ill-mannered white man from the West. Thailand is a monarchy and her constitution is modelled on Western democratic institutions. But in fact an unstable military dictatorship holds power; bloodless coups tend to occur every few years.

2. *Religious*. The state religion of Thailand is Theravada Buddhism, though there are tribal animists in the north and a predominantly Muslim-Malay population in the south. It is axiomatic that to be a good Thai one must be a Buddhist and the patriotism of anyone who forsakes Buddhism is somewhat suspect. Freedom of religious belief and practice, however, is allowed for in the constitution. But Buddhism is more than a religion; it is a culture and as such envelops and controls the whole of life from conception to cremation. The doctrines of Karma and rebirth make for a fatalistic view of existence; social rank or lack of it, financial security or poverty, mental ability or backwardness, health and beauty or sickness and deformity are all the predetermined and inevitable rewards of meritorious or evil deeds in a previous incarnation. The sincere Buddhist therefore is either a slave to a struggle to amass merit for himself and his parents with the constant fear of failure; or he is a victim of utter hopelessness and fear as to the future because his poverty, illness or deformity consign him to a beggar's status and deny him any chance of earning sufficient merit to improve his lot in a future rebirth.

3. *Economic*. Thailand's wealth lies in its high-quality rice, of which it has a huge surplus for export. But teak, rubber,

bamboo, jute, cotton, kapok, sugar, fruits, maize and meat, tin, precious stones and cement enable the country to support itself with a reasonably high standard of living. Her only imports are luxury items. But Thailand, to safeguard her future prosperity, needs to diversify her industries instead of relying so heavily on its overseas market for rice which could become smaller in the future.

4. *Christianity*. Christianity first reached Siam through Roman Catholic missionaries in the sixteenth and seventeenth centuries. The first permanent Protestant missionaries to the Thai arrived from America in 1831, though Karl Gutzlaff had spent three years there, from 1828 to 1831, during which time he translated the entire Bible into Thai. He won one Chinese to Christ and a Chinese church was organized in 1835 by the American Baptists. It was nineteen years, however, before the first Thai convert from Buddhism was baptized. Today, after more than one hundred years of Protestant missions, the Thai continue to reject Christianity and Thailand has the smallest percentage of Christians of any Asian country and any country in the world outside Muslim states, *i.e.* one in a thousand.

The Western missionary is given a characteristically polite welcome and attention is paid to what he has to say about Christ's free offer of salvation to man in his sinfulness and hope for eternity apart from hard-won human merit. Religiously self-satisfied Buddhists graciously approve his teaching as good but give it only second place to Buddhism, having no sense of sin or need. The poor are attracted by the message of hope, but few respond because of ancient national tradition and a lifetime of conditioning by the doctrine of endless reincarnation. Some lasting results have come from house-to-house visitation, children's meetings, radio broadcasts, literature distribution, tent campaigns and open-air film shows, but the soil generally remains hard and unyielding. Local churches are few in number and universally small in membership.

What methods would you use to effect a break-through in Thailand? (Discuss.)
Where the usual methods of evangelism employed by Western missionaries have met with little response, medical work seems

to have been the means of watering and softening the hard soil and preparing it to become receptive and fruitful. Christian hospitals have been a feature of missionary work in the north and in Bangkok for scores of years and more recently in the heart of Thailand's rice-growing region and in the Muslim south.

The Thai's fear of death which affects himself and his family makes him responsive to the Christian message of assurance of eternal life through faith when serious illness threatens his life and he turns to a Christian hospital. In ward services often led by Thai Christians the gospel is explained. Christian books and pamphlets made easily available are avidly read in the enforced leisure from busy lives. The first-class medical treatment together with the loving Christian care and at a nominal cost – Christianity in action – make a deep impression.

Does medical work create local churches?

Many patients who come from near and far return to their scattered towns and villages speaking highly of the Christian hospital and so ensure a welcome for future evangelistic visits. It is often in the homes of ex-patients that the evangelistic teams meet the sincere, and not merely the courteous, welcome, and such homes prove to be prepared soil in which the gospel seed sown by the evangelistic worker takes root and grows. Some who have already believed while in the hospital return home as ambassadors for Christ to win their neighbours. Thus small groups of Christians begin to meet. Local churches can and do result from general hospital work.

Leprosy clinics

But possibly the strongest churches in Central Thailand are the leprosy patient churches, which are the direct result of scores of monthly leprosy clinics. There thousands suffering from leprosy have been treated with the latest drugs and many have been cured. Those needing surgery benefit from the most modern techniques in plastic surgery and tendon transplants in the hands. Finally, rehabilitation schemes restore self-respect and send cured patients back into society with the means of livelihood. In the leprosy churches there are hundreds of patients and their relatives and friends who have responded to God's love and know in experience the assurance of eternal life now and hereafter. Thus compassion has touched the untouchable of Thailand and they follow Christ rejoicing. Again leprosy clinic work is an effective means of planting local churches.

The limitations

Hospitals in Thailand require a large number of nurse-aides and maintenance staff who are largely recruited locally. Of these only about 20% have been genuinely converted. Another 20% may profess conversion with a motive of pleasing the foreigner and so earning promotion or special privileges while leading double lives – 'Christians' while on their jobs, but anything but Christian in their local villages where their conduct brings the name of Christ into disrepute. The Thai are quick to detect mere sham. The remaining 60% are among those who, like the majority of Thai, make no response at all to the Christian message.

The local church in a hospital centre is inevitably almost entirely made up of hospital employees and foreign medical staff. Because the hospital staff often attracts the better educated, these tend to dominate the church life and organization and so to inhibit the development of local talent. So, should the hospital close down for any reason, the local church would disintegrate, being in effect merely a department of the hospital. To the hospital worker tied to his institution a limited view of his work can thus be very disappointing. For compensation he must look at the wider influence of the hospital.

Can you suggest ways in which these weaknesses can be overcome? (Discuss.)

7
Who goes into all the world?
the messengers needed

Manpower

In the foregoing chapters we have looked at the world and its needs, its growing population and increasing concentration of its people in urban communities. We have also thought with thanksgiving of the universal church and its current steady growth in some areas of the world. But environmentally speaking everything in the world today is antagonistic to the Christian gospel and consideration has been given to the problem of how, in a rapidly changing society, the world-wide responsibility of the church can most effectively be fulfilled. In a changing world the gospel remains unchanged, while man's need for the gospel is greater than ever. Moreover the tools for making the gospel known are more sophisticated than ever before. Finally, therefore, we find ourselves confronted with the crucial question of manpower.

In 1967 – the last year when the relevant statistics were available – in a world population of 3,280,000,000 the number of Protestants was 316,000,000, or rather less than 10%. Even if all of them were true Christians, that leaves an enormous number of people outside the Protestant church – just short of 3,000,000,000 in fact, with no knowledge at all of the gospel or with quite inadequate or erroneous ideas about God's way of salvation. 'How are they to hear without a preacher?' pleaded the apostle Paul.

Every Christian a witness

Quite clearly we must ponder these words in the context of a witnessing church. The church ought always to be a source of infection, a kind of epidemic or a 'plague', as the early church was said to be (Acts 24:5). A world-wide witnessing church will reach many millions through its own day-to-day activities and through the lives of church members in industry, in business, in education and, in the medical and social services – always supposing that every church member is an infectious witness, as he ought to be. *All* Christians are, by definition, witnesses. And every Christian should have a sense of vocation to his life's work. To this end every young Christian needs to be taught to make the matter of a career one for careful thought and prayer for guidance. However and wherever he or she spends their life, it ought to be with a deep sense of vocation and stewardship and indebtedness for the gifts and education received. 'We are debtors', or 'under obligation', says the apostle Paul in Romans 1, 'both to the wise and to the foolish.' This may all be too much to expect in an imperfect church, but this is precisely the way in which Christ communicates Himself to the world around through the church which is His Body. Probably the Moravian Church in its early days, with its emphasis on the total involvement of every member in evangelism, approximated most nearly to this ideal. 'Our Lord has given His church an assignment. Proclaiming the Gospel and gathering believers into reproducing churches are not optional activities; they are laid upon the people of the Great Redemption as something binding,' says Paul Rees.

Special envoys

But even granted the ideal, hundreds of millions would remain unaware of the truth that Christ died and rose again to save men from the guilt and penalty of their sins and to alleviate the social consequences of those sins. To meet this need our Lord is still pressing men and women of all nations into His service, and sending them out into all the world as His representatives. Those whom He sent in New Testament times were called 'apostles', or 'sent ones' (John 20:21, 22), which is also the meaning of the more modern and possibly obsolescent word 'missionaries' – people sent on a mission. (No prizes offered for an alternative title!)

Christ our King is still appointing His ambassadors throughout the world to act on His behalf in reconciling men to God (2 Corinthians 5:20). He needs His representatives both in the 'post-Christian' Western world of North America and Europe – not least in Great Britain – but also overseas where the need, as Bishop Stephen Neill has said, is always inevitably greater. He needs His ambassadors in the animistic world of Africa, in the Muslim world of North Africa and the Middle East, in the Hindu world of India and Ceylon, in the Buddhist world of Burma, Thailand and Japan, in the Roman Catholic world of Latin America and the Philippines, and not least in the Communist world. But that is not to say that these ambassadors should not be drawn from all countries of the world and from churches in the Third World as well as in the West.

In many capacities

In Old Testament times God called David, a shepherd boy, 'to fulfil all his will' and Amos, a herdsman, to proclaim His truth, as well as Elisha, the professional prophet. In the New Testament we find the apostle Paul spending a number of years as a teacher in the local church at Antioch before responding to God's call to the full-time and life-long task of evangelist and church-planter. Timothy was at first one of Paul's team of itinerant missionaries before he settled down into a local pastorate. Mark had a brief missionary career with Paul and 'Uncle' Barnabas before returning to Jerusalem a chastened missionary 'drop-out' who later became 'profitable' to the apostle. Titus too was an itinerant evangelist before becoming the senior pastor of the churches in Crete. Luke was a medical man with literary gifts who frequently accompanied Paul on his journeys and was the author of the third Gospel and the historian of the early church, a part-time missionary, part-time professional.

Subsequently history abounds in men and women who followed in the steps of these New Testament witnesses: Patrick, who evangelized Ireland and Scotland; Augustine, who brought the gospel to the pagan English; the Nestorian Christians, who took the good news to China in the sixth century; Matteo Ricci, who established the church in Peking in the sixteenth century; Francis Xavier, who proclaimed Christ in India,

South-East Asia and Japan in the same century; William Carey, the printer-linguist; Robert Morrison, a servant of the East India Company and the translator of the Chinese Bible; Sir Robert Bowring, Governor of Hongkong and British Ambassador to Siam, who composed the hymn 'In the cross of Christ I glory'; and General Gordon of Khartoum, who, as a professional soldier, was not ashamed to own his Lord in Egypt and China. More recently Admirals Stileman and Startin and Generals Dobbie and Arthur-Smith have witnessed for Christ all over the world in war and in peace. Among our contemporaries who are making a significant contribution to evangelism and the growth of the churches are a British doctor in Formosa, a British businessman in Ghana, university lecturers in Singapore, through whom the IVF work was established there, and many others in so-called 'secular employment'. So God commissions His witnesses, but in varying capacities.

Life-time service

Past history, however, makes it clear that the pioneers of the church in every continent were almost always those who had dedicated their whole lives to the task. They toiled to acquire the language and then to give the Bible in that language to the people. They integrated themselves into the culture of their adopted land. In Thailand they laboured nineteen years before the first convert was baptized and in Central Celebes seventeen years. Only then could they begin the slow task of church building. The first Lisu converts in Thailand were baptized at Easter 1970 after nineteen years of work.

Whether in Africa or Asia the initial task demanded all their strength and all their time and all their lives. Nothing less was even contemplated when they gave themselves to God for 'missionary service'. For them, discipleship involved forsaking all for Christ's sake – possessions, home, loved ones – and living sacrificially for the rest of their days, usually in privation and comparative poverty. 'If Jesus Christ be God and He died for me,' wrote C. T. Studd, the wealthy London socialite and England cricketer, before going to China as a missionary, 'then no sacrifice can be too great for me to make for Him.' But in our day, with exciting, challenging and potentially lucrative vocations awaiting them, many young people find that giving up the good life to prepare themselves to 'sell people overseas on a Christ they do not want' is just not worth the sacrifice, especially if you can serve mankind and have governments pay the bill.

But the world's present need urgently requires a category of overseas witnesses prepared to be cross-bearing disciples of Jesus Christ. They are certainly not redundant or out-dated; it is definitely not a greater service to God to go into business, as is sometimes suggested. Lesslie Newbigin, in *One Body, One Gospel, One World,* says that 'there is something spiritually precious in the traditional conception of life-long missionary service which ought not to be lightly cast away. In holding out before each generation of young people the call to a life-long and total commitment, missions have been doing something which was not merely practically important for the work of foreign missions but also of the deepest value to the whole life of the churches.' After all, Christ's call to His disciples to forsake all and follow Him in a life of self-renunciation and cross-bearing is as impelling and mandatory today as in the days of the apostles.

Moreover the overseas churches are saying plainly that they welcome full-time missionaries, especially those who are prepared to integrate their life and witness completely with that of the local churches. This is the traditional image of the missionary: 'a disciple of Jesus Christ who serves his Lord in an area not of his own choosing, and undertakes a life of witness in seeking to win men and women for the Lord Jesus Christ and to build them up in grace and fellowship, solely out of constraint by the love of Christ and in obedience to the will of God for him.' To this definition of what a missionary is we would add that in the contemporary situation the missionary is essentially 'a servant' of the churches and not, as formerly, their overseer. Like his Lord he must gladly wear the apron of a slave (1 Peter 5:5).

Missionary societies
Normally such men and women, if they did not found missionary societies, as did Henry Venn, Hudson Taylor, C. T.

Studd, *etc.*, were members of such societies. A missionary society was then, and still seems to be in the 1970s, a necessary link between churches at home and churches abroad. 'It is the means whereby the local church at home can discharge its God-given responsibility in world-mission and those from within the fellowship of the local church can serve with others of similar calling' (*i.e.* in world outreach).

It is perhaps important here to say that in the New Testament sense no 'denomination' is properly speaking 'a church'. A denomination is an association of numerous local churches that follow similar recognizable patterns of church life and worship. But independent local churches are no less churches than those within a historic denomination, provided the Word and the Sacraments have their right place. Historically, each 'denomination' has had its own missionary society or societies. But missionary societies are no substitute for the church. They are certainly not themselves a church. Despite common practice they have no authority to commission and send out workers. According to early church precedent only the church, the local church, has such authority (Acts 13:1–3). But societies do provide a necessary fellowship with common aims and a common goal – that of planting and establishing churches (though not reproducing Western denominations!). And even when, eventually, individual members of the society are able to integrate themselves completely into the life of the autonomous and indigenous churches and the missionary structures which have hitherto functioned overseas can be dismantled, there will still be a need for some missionary organization structure at the home end to channel information, mobilize prayer support and select the workers requested by the overseas churches.

Meanwhile the missionary societies are providing extremely valuable service agencies for the overseas churches – a reserve of experts in various spheres of Christian work upon which the churches can draw, as they have need, to supplement their own lack of personnel. In this way they are demonstrating their desire for a far closer co-operation and identification with the national churches of the world. That integration is long overdue in the case of the advanced churches of India, for instance. It is essential in Indonesia, where many workers can enter only on these terms, and are personally sponsored and invited by local churches or church institutions. But in many cases the national churches are so new, so small and so immature that they would not know what to do with foreigners who offered to become church members and to work under their direction. Church/mission co-operation or integration is therefore largely a matter of timing.

In these rapidly changing times it is urgent to lower the age of mission administrators, to effect mergers where possible, to rotate home and field leadership, to educate the supporting constituencies, to share the common problems and ensure that mission leaders are widely read and instructed in developments outside their own spheres of activity.

Perhaps the analogy of the modern, highly-trained regular army is useful. Advertisements invite young men to 'join the professionals'. Should we not be thinking ahead in terms of a smaller, full-time, highly trained force of people prepared to give long periods of their lives to overseas service, using cheaper air passages for more frequent home leave and for visits to their children? The problem of their children's education, which faces all married missionaries, has always been acute and is no less so in these days of specialized education. Normally the full-time 'professional' is more effective in relation to the end in view than others. But this 'professional' category must also be matched with two other categories of Christian workers to produce a balanced fighting force.

Short-term service

The Voluntary Service Overseas and the Peace Corps organizations have attracted thousands of British and American young people with a spirit of adventure and a desire to serve in a temporary capacity all over the world. Many have given valuable service in a short time, though there have also been not a few failures, largely through lack of proper orientation at the outset. Increasingly, in areas where English is commonly used and where there is therefore no language barrier, missions are encouraging people to undertake short-term service. Youth workers, technicians, medical specialists and teachers are giving valuable temporary service. Such service has sometimes proved to be a stepping-stone to more permanent service, having given the short-termer a first-hand acquaintance with missionary work as it really is.

Secular employment overseas

For many years Christians have been going overseas in government service, as administrators, educators, engineers and agriculturalists, or with aid organizations like the Overseas Development Corporation and the Colombo Plan, as well as with commercial firms having agencies abroad. Some 15,000 British Christians are working overseas in one or other of the above capacities. To witness as a Christian in those circumstances has often been a spiritually lonely task and many have failed to be effective witnesses; some have even become spiritual casualties, as happens also among their missionary colleagues, with less excuse. Others, however, have made a major contribution to the upbuilding of the churches even in a comparatively short space of time. Such people can often witness in spheres not easily penetrated by the 'professionals' who, in some circumstances, especially in Muslim lands, find themselves in a terrible blind alley where only the man who is serving the country while serving Christ has a valid and proper relation to the people. Evangelical work in the Argentine was pioneered by English lay Christians working on the railways; today Buenos Aires alone has eighty Brethren Assemblies as a result. In the case of Afghanistan one 'non-professional' has maintained a witness for many years and so prepared the way for the present entry of Christian medical teams at the invitation of the Afghan government, on similar terms to the United Mission to Nepal.

As, in the future, some countries may exclude the 'professionals', the importance of the CSOs (Christians in Service Overseas) may increase, though so far such people have not been able to do anything in countries from which the 'professionals' have already been excluded, *e.g.* China, Burma or Southern Sudan.

CSOs have the advantage of being no charge on sparse missionary budgets, but at the same time their very status and living standards tend to remove them from close contact with the ordinary man in the street and preclude much cultural integration with the people. It is clearly an advantage for them to be linked with the missionaries working in the area, perhaps as 'associates', for the sake of the fellowship and prayer support they can thus share. And some societies have already welcomed such associates into a formal relationship.

In some cases university lecturers have found it preferable to go overseas as full members of a missionary society, which then seconds them to universities in their area, as in the case of a geography lecturer in Java and a physics lecturer in Sumatra. In other situations, such an association with a society might be undesirable.

No-one contemplating this form of service should overlook the fact that a CSO normally has only his spare time for Christian work, and in some situations a too-active witness would not meet with official favour. Moreover, few remain posted to one place for long. Like their 'professional' colleagues they should be identified as closely as possible with the local church (where such exists) and render their service in the context of the local church. On this ground, *i.e.* relationship to the local church, missionaries and non-missionaries stand in an identical relationship and their respective spheres of service are thus entirely complementary.

Arthur F. Glasser sums up the need of the world in these words: 'We can expect God to continue to call not a few top-quality Christians and train them by His Spirit to serve His people throughout the world. They will need more devotion to His Son, more loyalty to His truth, more theological sensitivity, more language skill, more thirst for intercultural and ecumenical experience, more energy and finally, more evidence of possessing a "spiritual gift", to confirm God's call and guarantee potential usefulness in His service.'

'World evangelization is in part an exercise in logistics – getting forces to the place where they are needed in time' (Malcolm Bradshaw, *East Asia Millions*, 1968). 'The great need is for a new mobility, a new freedom to use the entire resources of the church for fresh advance into the unevangelized areas of mankind' (Lesslie Newbigin, *One Body, One Gospel, One World*). Nothing less is demanded than the total mobilization of the church's manpower to serve both at home and overseas in carrying out the Divine plan.

Training essential

The present-day task of all Christian workers overseas is much more complex than that of the early pioneers, and in The colonial period of foreign missions. Instead of witnessing, as at one time, to people, the majority of whom were illiterates, the missionary will often find himself among well-educated people, possibly better educated than himself. Instead of trying to make an impression on the virgin minds of primitive people, he will sometimes be attempting to convince people with philosophical backgrounds and already familiar with Marxist ideas. Instead of positioning himself under the traditional palm-tree to preach, he will need to declare his faith on the factory floor, in the busy streets and amid the bright lights of big cities, or even in a lecture room confronted with rowdy revolutionary students. Instead of coping with the elementary problems of small village churches, he may have to contend with the complexities and headaches of large city churches.

If, therefore, thorough missionary training was found desirable in the past, it is even more necessary today. It is not enough to have a university degree and to have qualified in physics, history or modern languages. Christian workers overseas today need to be equally well qualified in theology, philosophy, sociology and church administration. At the very least they must have a more-than-average working knowledge of Scripture and the ability to teach and handle the Word of God effectively. No training can be too thorough if one is to become a worthy colleague and servant of the churches overseas and to earn their respect and confidence. The CSOs too need as much training as they can fit in, if they are to be really effective witnesses.

While training is acknowledged as essential for all going overseas, the length of time cannot be categorically laid down. Training should be 'tailor-made' for the individual, to fit his particular background and needs. But even formal training is not in itself adequate preparation to meet the severe demands of Christian service abroad today. All would-be workers abroad must have a working faith in the Person and work of the Holy

Spirit, without which neither the church nor the individual can fulfil the task of taking the gospel to the ends of the earth (Acts 1:8). At home the Holy Spirit's energizing is equally necessary for those whose ministry is to intercede and to provide the essential finance.

Sharing Christ's compassion

An earlier generation of students was fired with an intense love for Christ and a flaming desire to be abandoned to the will of God in relation to world evangelization. They shared in an obvious way the compassion of Christ for a lost world. In one sense everything has changed since those days. In another sense nothing has changed. The church's task is far from complete and her responsibility remains very great and very grave. Nor have our Lord's conditions of discipleship ever been watered down, despite the immense changes in living conditions which missionaries frequently enjoy today. 'Carry no purse', said Jesus, yet we now command comfortable salaries which enable us to maintain our homeside living standards; 'no bag, no sandals', but now we all have our powerful cars and electric refrigerators; 'and salute no one on the road', and yet some of today's missionaries have time and to spare for social life of every kind. These things may not be wrong in themselves and may even be necessary in our present-day world, but the principles of discipleship remain unchanged. Where today can we find that costly sacrifice which has been the hall-mark of true discipleship all down the ages?

The hour is late; all human society is in crisis. The forces opposed to Christ and the gospel seem to grow stronger and more aggressive every day. Is it already too late? No, for the note of certainty as to ultimate triumph runs right through the Scriptures. We must not measure tomorrow's advances by yesterday's defeats. Jesus Christ is already crowned and exalted. One day the hostile world and its rulers must acknowledge His Lordship and Kingship and bow the knee in submission (Philippians 2:10, 11). The kingdoms of the world are destined to become the Kingdom of our Lord and of His Christ. The task of world evangelization is no lost cause. It is the only cause in the world today which must succeed, because it is the cause of God Himself and of His Son who declared that all authority was His, on earth as well as in heaven.

But those who would share in the coming victory must first share in the cross, loving not their lives even unto death (Revelation 12:11). If we suffer with Him, we shall also reign with Him. The time for reigning will be through eternity. The time for suffering and serving is now.

BIBLIOGRAPHY

The Making of a Missionary by Douglas N. Sargent (Hodder and Stoughton, 1960).

Give Up Your Small Ambitions by Michael Griffiths (Inter-Varsity Press, 1970).

Customs, Culture and Christianity by Eugene A. Nida (Tyndale Press, 1963).

Time for Action by A. J. Broomhall (Inter-Varsity Press, 1965).

World Missions Handbook (Evangelical Missionary Alliance, 1969. New edition in preparation).

Problems to ponder
How to cope with 'closed doors'

Background situation

North Africa has been a Muslim stronghold for nearly 2,000 years.

Fifteen years ago, Tunisia, Algeria and Morocco were subject to French rule in varying degrees. Autonomy came to Tunisia and Morocco in 1956 and to Algeria after a bloody struggle in 1961.

Independence has been followed by a drive in favour of Arabization and Islamization.

North Africa in 1972 is an arena in which conflicting ideologies struggle for first place; Islam frantically tries to maintain its traditional position through religious and social institutions, while nationalistic socialism in Libya and Algeria and rank materialism in Morocco fight for supremacy.

In the urban populations of North Africa there is an 'ideological void' caused by religious and political thought on an international scale. Television, the desire to learn English and the popular magazines all mark an international awareness.

Church situation

Christian churches are comparatively few and Christians are few in number and face fierce opposition from the Muslim authorities, especially in the rural areas. But local groups of believers exist in most of the main cities of North Africa and a few of them are organized churches with office-bearing elders.

The objective

To preach Christ, to make disciples, to establish indigenous local churches and to act as counsellors (rather than leaders) to those churches.

The difficulties

1. Though religious liberty is provided for in the Constitution, no religion but Islam has liberty for religious propaganda and apostasy from Islam is barely tolerated.

2. North African governments are becoming less tolerant of Christian missions and no missionary society in Morocco has had legal rights of operation since 1965. Many missionaries have already been expelled and withdrawn to Marseilles from Algeria and Morocco.

3. Colportage is no longer possible in Morocco, though two bookshops miraculously remain open. The Bible societies face severe import restrictions and distribution difficulties.

So what would you advise to be done? (Discuss.)

Possible courses of action

Methods are necessarily changing rapidly. The old traditional 'mission station' or 'compound' is a thing of the past. From a 'station' type of work, a change is being made to a ministry in the context of a secular job. Flexibility is the key-word. Those who are able to remain are continuing their witness within the framework of the Ministries of Education or Health, serving as English teachers, doctors, nurses and midwives or in business. One couple manages a hotel in Morocco, while another in Tunis was employed by the Berlitz School of Languages and was offered the post of Director. All remain committed to the task of preaching Christ and making disciples.

For those forced to leave North Africa, the following activities are now paramount:

1. Bible correspondence courses in French and Arabic from the Radio School of the Bible in Marseilles or from Malaga in Spain bring the majority of new contacts. Follow up is done by special service workers in Morocco.

2. Radio broadcasting to North Africa over Trans World Radio and ELWA in Liberia. This is expensive, and more effective medium-wave coverage and greater co-operation between Arabic-speaking broadcasters is urgent.

3. Some missionaries expelled from North Africa are now reaching North Africans elsewhere. One couple refused residence in Morocco is now working among the 800,000 North Africans – mostly Algerians – in the south of France.

4. One lady forced to leave Morocco obtained entry to Eastern Algeria to do intensive follow-up work among teen-age girls. But there are other valuable opportunities in a variety of secular occupations:

1. A keen evangelical French physicist is on the faculty of Science in Algiers where a Christian student centre has a useful ministry. Another such centre is planned for Tunis.

2. A missionary who speaks fluent Arabic transferred from Morocco to Tunis to study at the University there. Later, with a Master's degree, she expects to return as a university staff member.

3. Eight former missionaries have re-entered Tunisia as students of Arabic, but each will need to establish himself in a professional capacity if he is to remain there.

4. Another missionary expelled from Algeria studied constructional engineering in Marseilles and was offered a post with a French constructional company in their North Africa extension programme.

In all these cases, the home of the Christian worker is the chief sphere of ministry, as any witness on the job must be very discreet.

Conclusion

'Closed doors' do not release a missionary society from its mandate in any area of the world. In North Africa the church of Jesus Christ is called to fulfil its mission by preaching the Word of reconciliation. The conflict on earth is catching the rhythm of the struggle in heavenly places. Increased opportunities in North Africa have provoked increased opposition. Today North Africa is having its day of unparalleled opportunity and so the principal evangelical thrust must be maintained so long as front, side and back doors remain open to the ambassadors of the cross.

A note on the statistical tables

It is impossible to compile statistical tables of this nature which will be mutually compatible. It would be ideal to have all the figures relating to the same year, but at the moment this is not a realistic goal. Statistics are collected in different ways in different countries, and in some there are governmental pressures at work to produce results which 'look right'. Equally the statistics of numbers of Christians are subject to a variety of church definitions: there is no division made between nominal and committed members.

Such difficulties tempt many to abandon the idea of basing anything on statistics, but no discussion of strategy can be complete without some factual basis. The figures quoted in these lists have been drawn from two major sources in order to achieve some degree of uniformity: Columns 2–4: *The World Bank Atlas* of population, per capita product and growth rates, 1970. This uses figures for 1968, largely derived from the *UN Statistical Yearbook*. Columns 1, 5–8: *World Christian Handbook*, 1968 Edition, using figures ranging from 1962 to 1966.

The two groups are thus slightly out of phase, but a simple calculation based on column 3 will give the correction for population at the time of the church figures. A new edition of the *World Christian Handbook* is scheduled for 1972, when the reader will be able to update his figures. Reference may also be made to *The Statesman's Yearbook* (Macmillan), and the *Britannica Yearbooks*, which are also useful sources of general data on world population and general religious divisions.

Whilst emphasizing the fact that statistics must be used with care, therefore, it is also important that any planning should use what figures are available. More accurate details can often be obtained for smaller areas from the embassies of the countries concerned, or through missionary societies.

Special points

1. All the world is the mission field: so every country is included.

2. The percentage increase of population is given as the average of the increases from 1961 to 1968. It is instructive to compare the European averages with those of, say, South America, Japan and Australia.

3. The Gross National Product per head of the population gives some indication of the national wealth and the standards of living available to the population as a whole. In every country there are the rich and the poor, but a smaller proportion of rich can be supported by a country with a low GNP.

4. The figures for Protestant and Roman Catholic 'communities' have been chosen rather than the figures for actual church members of committed, active Christians. It is impossible to arrive at any really satisfactory figure here, and the purpose of these figures is to highlight the general situation. Even where the Protestant community is relatively large it will include a large proportion of formal adherents.

5. The definition of a full-time worker varies from place to place. In general it includes lay, as well as ordained, workers. The figures for the European and Australasian areas are combined, since few of these countries have foreign workers.

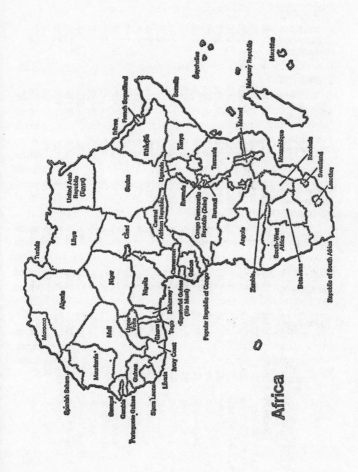

Africa

131

AFRICA	Area (000 sq mi)	Population 1968 (000)	% increase per year 1961-68	GNP per head (US $)	Protestant community (000)	RC community (000)	Protestant full-time National workers	Protestant full-time Foreign workers	Number of people per Protestant worker
Nigeria	357	62,650	2.4	70	2,524	2,250	11,681	650	5,080
United Arab Rep.	386	31,693	2.5	170	149	162	1,048	75	28,222
Ethiopia/Eritrea	395	24,212	2.0	70	227	125	2,320	900	7,520
South Africa/S.W. Africa	780	19,781	2.3	650	10,021	1,263	19,316	2,770	895
Zaire	895	16,730	2.1	90	2,106	5,650	24,200	1,057	662
Sudan	968	14,770	2.9	100	166	415	737	32	19,207
Morocco	171	14,580	2.9	190	6	400	9	66	194,400
Algeria	919	12,943	2.3	220	1	500	30	50	161,788
Tanzania	362	12,508	2.5	80	1,034	2,400	5,575	734	1,983
Kenya	225	10,209	2.9	130	788	1,050	5,266	889	1,659
Ghana	92	8,376	2.7	170	687	740	2,478	210	3,116
Uganda	94	8,133	2.5	110	1,521	2,250	374	178	14,787
Mozambique	298	7,274	1.3	200	126	895	2,760	111	2,534
Malagasy	229	6,500	2.4	100	1,113	910	3,650	167	1,703
Cameroun	167	5,590	2.2	140	702	950	4,950	295	1,066
Angola	471	5,362	1.3	190	350	1,915	2,160	90	2,383
Upper Volta	106	5,175	2.2	50	30	180	288	96	13,477
Rhodesia	150	4,940	3.2	220	598	335	7,194	830	616
Mali	464	4,787	2.1	90	7	31	108	120	20,996
Tunisia	48	4,660	2.3	220	2	40	0	5	932,000
Malawi	46	4,270	2.6	50	635	580	1,550	257	2,363

Ivory Coast	126	4,100	2·8	260	97	280	366	190	7,374
Zambia	208	4,065	3·0	220	229	550	1,972	550	1,612
Niger	489	3,806	3·6	70	1	32	0	97	39,237
Guinea	96	3,795	2·7	90	2	28	7	60	56,642
Senegal	78	3,685	2·1	170	2	147	0	38	96,974
Chad	495	3,460	1·5	60	94	89	770	166	3,697
Burundi	11	3,406	2·0	50	226	1,570	1,345	100	2,263
Rwanda	10	3,405	3·1	70	171	800	2,000	77	1,639
Somalia	246	2,747	4·0	60	0·1	8	5	57	44,306
Dahomey	44	2,571	2·9	80	34	300	126	52	14,444
Sierra Leone	28	2,475	1·3	150	77	32	800	175	2,538
Libya	679	1,803	3·7	1,020	2	40	0	8	225,375
Togo	22	1,769	2·6	100	97	265	300	45	5,128
Central African Rep.	238	1,488	2·4	120	146	180	720	234	1,560
Liberia	43	1,130	1·7	210	120	14	900	353	902
Mauritania	419	1,120	1·8	180	0	0	0	0	—
Lesotho	12	910	2·9	80	244	322	740	22	1,194
Congo—Popular Rep.	139	870	1·5	230	148	320	1,443	100	564
Botswana	275	600	3·0	100	101	8	70	32	5,882
Portuguese Guinea	14	529	0·2	230	1	27	0	21	25,194
Gabon	102	480	0·9	310	81	234	286	60	1,387
Swaziland	7	395	2·8	200	26	28	537	90	630
Gambia	4	350	2·0	100	6	6	14	3	20,588
Equatorial Guinea	11	281	1·8	260	6	0	53	14	4,194
French Somaliland	8	84	1·4	620	9	0	0	0	—
Spanish Sahara	116	48	2·0	240	0	0	0	0	—

Central America and the Caribbean

Gulf of Mexico

U.S.A.

Bahama Islands

Caicos Is.

Turks Is.

Cuba

Cayman Is.

Haiti

Jamaica

British Honduras

Mexico

Guatemala

Honduras

El Salvador

Nicaragua

Costa Rica

Dominican Republic

Puerto Rico

Anguilla

Antigua

Montserrat

Guadeloupe

St. Christophers

Nevis

Dominica

Martinique

St. Lucia

Barbados

St. Vincent

Grenada

Tobago

Trinidad

Caribbean Sea

Curacao

Aruba

Bonaire

Canal Zone

Panama

134

Venezuela
Guyana
Surinam
French Guiana
Colombia
Ecuador
Peru
Brazil
Bolivia
Paraguay
Chile
Argentina
Uruguay

South
America

Falkland Islands

AMERICAS

	Area (000 sq ml)	Population 1968 (000)	% Increase per year 1961-68	GNP per head (US $)	Protestant community (000)	RC community (000)	Protestant full-time National workers	Protestant full-time Foreign workers	Number of people per Protestant worker
USA	3,549	201,152	1·4	3,980	65,476	44,000	318,165	1,730	555
Brazil	3,286	88,209	1·6	820	7,923	70,200	27,300	255	3,038
Mexico	762	47,627	3·5	530	702	35,000	5,734	515	7,952
Argentina	1,084	23,617	1·6	820	530	20,400	1,225	180	13,573
Canada	3,560	20,772	1·9	2,460	6,521	7,900	16,122	405	1,274
Colombia	455	20,043	3·2	310	111	15,000	530	460	21,436
Peru	496	12,772	3·1	380	128	10,500	1,230	290	7,557
Venezuela	352	9,686	3·5	950	52	7,750	360	330	14,901
Chile	286	9,351	2·5	480	881	6,700	650	300	9,542
Cuba	44	8,270	2·4	310	296	6,000	660	320	8,615
Ecuador	106	5,695	3·4	220	19	4,380	265	160	9,735
Guatemala	42	4,864	3·1	320	131	4,230	1,080	540	3,923
Bolivia	424	4,680	2·6	150	67	3,600	850	700	3,367
Haiti	11	4,671	2·0	70	501	2,900	970	155	2,797
Dominican Rep.	19	4,029	3·6	290	77	3,350	590	53	5,408
El Salvador	8	3,267	3·6	280	75	2,100	1,280	120	2,450
Uruguay	72	2,818	1·3	520	40	2,220	280	100	7,045
Puerto Rico	3	2,723	1·8	1,340	194	2,300	790	190	3,060
Honduras	43	2,413	3·4	260	57	1,500	430	175	3,892
Paraguay	407	2,231	3·1	230	19	1,850	250		5,249
Jamaica	4	1,908	2·0	460	755	130	1,350	386	1,099

Nicaragua	57	1,848	3·4	370	54	1,350	300	68	5,022
Costa Rica	20	1,650	3·5	450	39	970	260	130	4,231
Panama	29	1,372	3·3	580	57	1,130	290	150	3,118
Trinidad/Tobago	2	1,021	2·6	870	375	340	1,020	140	880
Guyana	83	719	3·1	340	475	?	920	115	694
Surinam	63	375	3·5	430	64	66	80	50	2,885
Guadeloupe	0·7	321	2·1	510	67	?	140	60	1,605
Barbados	0·2	252	1·0	440	237	307	234	25	973
Netherlands Antilles	0·4	215	1·4	1,200	6	145	28	30	3,707
Bahamas	4	177	5·8	1,460	88	27	400	50	393
British Honduras	9	116	3·1	390	34	64	75	30	1,105
St Lucia	0·2	108	2·9	220	335	?	250	80	327
St Vincent	0·2	93	2·9	210	see PANAMA				
Canal Zone	0·6	60	4·5	1,810	see PANAMA				
Bermuda	0·02	50	1·6	2,670	22	4	30	8	1,316
French Guiana	23	40	2·1	890	0·5	32	1	0	40,000

ASIA	Area (000 sq ml)	Population 1968 (000)	% Increase per year 1961-68	GNP per head (US $)	Protestant community (000)	RC community (000)	Protestant full-time National workers	Protestant full-time Foreign workers	Number of people per Protestant worker
China	3,708	730,000	1·5	90	est. 700	est. 2,200	est. 10,000	0	73,000
India	1,262	532,000	2·5	100	5,303	6,625	25,179	3,514	18,541
Pakistan/Bangladesh	366	123,163	2·6	100	473	341	2,850	450	37,322
Indonesia	575	113,720	2·4	100	4,371	1,575	16,831	575	6,533
Japan	143	101,090	1·0	1,190	818	315	6,400	1,860	12,238
Philippines	116	35,883	3·4	180	4,195	23,000	12,472	834	2,697
Thailand	198	33,693	3·1	150	31	116	300	240	62,394
Turkey	301	33,550	2·5	310	10	20	3	2	6,710,000
Korea (South)	38	30,470	2·7	180	1,873	650	3,520	658	7,293
Iran	627	27,150	3·0	310	8	21	74	43	223,504
Burma	262	26,353	2·1	70	785	222	2,650	71	9,685
Vietnam (North)	63	20,700	3·2	90	?	est. 680	450	?	—
Vietnam (South)	66	17,414	2·7	130	56	1,600	450	170	28,087
Afghanistan	250	16,113	2·0	80	No reliable statistics				—
Taiwan (Formosa)	14	13,466	3·0	270	459	266	2,580	570	4,275
Korea (North)	45	13,000	2·6	250	No reliable statistics	see INDIA			—
Ceylon	25	11,970	2·4	180	89	720	631	73	17,003
Nepal	55	10,652	1·8	80	0·5	0·5	14	29	247,721
Malaysia	129	10,386	3·1	330	197	265	2,240	476	3,825
Iraq	169	8,634	2·8	260	5	125	70	43	76,407

Country									
Saudi Arabia	927	7,112	1·7	360	No reliable statistics		?	15	—
Khmer Republic	71	7,087	3·4	120	2	55	166	30	29,087
Syria	71	5,701	2·8	210	17	251	0	2	2,720,000
Yemen	75	5,440	2·1	70	0·01	0	1,200	420	2,424
Hong Kong	0·4	3,927	3·1	710	171	215	0	31	91,129
Laos	89	2,825	2·4	100	4	27	30	110	19,607
Israel	8	2,745	3·3	1,360	16	76	250	190	5,864
Lebanon	3	2,580	2·6	560	11	650	175	77	8,345
Jordan	37	2,103	2·7	260		16			
Singapore	0·2	1,988	2·5	700	see MALAYSIA				
Mongolia	684	1,210	3·0	430	No reliable statistics		10	30	29,875
South Yemen	62	1,195	2·3	120	1	10			
Bhutan	18	810	2·0	60	No reliable statistics				
Muscat & Oman	48	565	0·0	250	see SOUTH YEMEN				
Kuwait	9	540	8·7	3,540	4	5	2	6	67,500
Bahrein	0·2	200	3·7	390	see SOUTH YEMEN		?		
Sikkim	3	187	2·0	70	? see INDIA			?	
Trucial Oman	32	133	3·9	1,920	see SOUTH YEMEN				

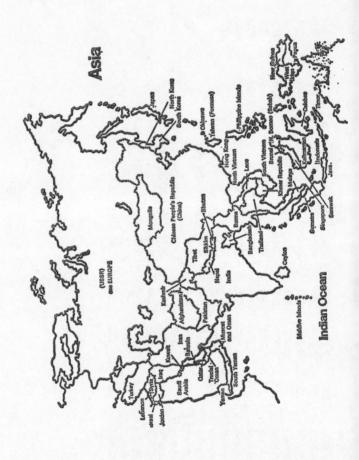

Asia

North Korea
Japan
South Korea
Okinawa
Taiwan (Formosa)
Hong Kong
Philippine Islands
North Vietnam
Laos
South Vietnam
Brunei
N. Borneo (Sabah)
Kalimantan
Khmer Republic
Malaya
Indonesia
Sumatra
Singapore
Java
Sarawak
New Guinea
Celebes
Timor

Mongolia

Chinese People's Republic (China)

Bhutan
Tibet
Sikkim
Nepal
Burma
Bangladesh
Thailand
India
Ceylon

(USSR)
see EUROPE

Kashmir
Afghanistan
Pakistan
Iran
Muscat and Oman
Bahrein

Maldive Islands

Indian Ocean

Turkey
Lebanon
Israel
Syria
Jordan
Iraq
Kuwait
Qatar
Trucial Oman
Saudi Arabia
Yemen
South Yemen

Australasia

West Samoa
Amer. Samoa
Tonga
Gilbert and Ellice Is.
Fiji
British Solomon Is.
New Hebrides
New Caledonia
New Zealand
West Irian
New Guinea
Papua
Australia
Tasmania

	Area (000 sq mi)	Population 1968 (000)	% increase per year 1961-68	GNP per head (US $)	Protestant community (000)	RC community (000)	Protestant full-time workers	Number of people per Protestant worker
AUSTRAL-ASIA, PACIFIC								
Australia	2,968	12,031	2·0	2,071	6,738	2,590	12,980	927
New Zealand	104	2,828	2·2	2,000	1,720	365	1,935	1,461
Papua, New Guinea	176	2,300	2·4	210	568	440	2,360	975
Fiji	7	505	3·1	330	157	35	1,100	459
Brit. Solomon Is.	12	148	2·1	200	134	—	2,360	63
West. Samoa	1	137	2·7	130	89	33	400	342
Fr. Polynesia	4	100	2·8	1,420	42	27	62	1,613
Guam	0·2	100	5·3	1,790	2	55	25	4,000
New Caledonia	7	96	2·6	1,720	16	61	100	960
Tonga	0·3	81	3·2	300	54	12	530	153
New Hebrides	6	78	2·1	390	65	11	890	88
Gilbert & Ellice Is.	0·3	54	2·0	400	27	23	175	309
Amer. Samoa	0·1	31	5·6	550	see WESTERN SAMOA			
EUROPE & USSR								
USSR	8,650	237,798	1·3	1,110	56,724°	3,000	450	528,440
Germany (Fed. Rep.)	96	60,165	1·0	1,970	45,177†	27,500†	27,440	2,193
UK	89	55,283	0·7	1,790	33,556	5,300	51,400	1,076

Italy	116	52,750	0·8	1,230	183	46,300	1,035	50,966
France	213	49,920	1·1	2,130	725	39,500	1,840	27,130
Spain	504	32,621	0·9	730	43	31,200	250	130,484
Poland	120	32,305	1·1	880	464	28,000	720	44,868
Yugoslavia	99	20,154	1·1	510	156	6,125	325	62,012
Romania	114	19,721	0·9	780	1,209	2,700	1,690	1,167
Germany (Dem. Rep.)	42	17,084	−0·1	1,430	see GERMANY (FED. REP.)			—
Czechoslovakia	49	14,362	0·6	1,240	1,947	6,900	2,700	5,319
Netherlands	13	12,725	1·3	1,620	4,652	4,810	3,950	3,221
Hungary	36	10,255	0·3	980	2,443	6,000	3,290	3,117
Belgium	12	9,619	0·6	1,810	34	8,700	280	34,354
Portugal	35	9,465	0·9	460	33	8,600	184	51,440
Greece	51	8,803	0·9	740	7,519*	46	12,000	734
Bulgaria	43	8,370	0·8	770	34	32	70	119,571
Sweden	174	7,918	0·7	2,620	7,633	34	8,400	943
Austria	32	7,350	0·5	1,320	498	6,410	545	13,468
Switzerland	16	6,147	1·7	2,490	2,605	2,500	1,670	3,681
Denmark	17	4,870	0·8	2,070	4,570	27	2,350	2,072
Finland	305	4,689	0·7	1,720	4,412	2	5,700	823
Norway	125	3,819	0·8	2,000	3,658	8	1,840	2,076
Ireland	27	2,910	0·3	980	10	2,673	15	194,000
Albania	11	2,019	2·9	400	?	75	?	—
Luxembourg	1	336	0·9	2,170	6	309	11†	30,545
Iceland	40	201	1·7	1,680	179	1	190	1,058

NB * Includes Orthodox Church † all Germany.

Europe

Iceland

Ireland

UK

Norway

Sweden

Finland

Denmark

Netherlands

Belgium

Luxembourg

Germany (Dem.Rep.)

Germany (Fed.Rep.)

Poland

Czechoslovakia

Austria

Hungary

Switzerland

France

Spain

Portugal

Italy

Yugoslavia

Albania

Romania

Bulgaria

Greece

USSR